**Approaches to participation
in rural development**

Approaches to participation in rural development

Peter Oakley and David Marsden

Published on behalf of the ACC
Task Force on Rural Development

International Labour Office   Geneva

ISBN 92-2-103594-8

First published 1984
Sixth impression 1990

Printed in the German Democratic Republic   ZIM

PREFACE

This study was carried out at the request of the Panel on People's Participation. The Panel itself was established in 1981 by the Inter-Agency Task Force on Rural Development, chaired by Professor Nurul Islam, Assistant Director-General of the Food and Agriculture Organization of the United Nations. The creation of the Panel on People's Participation reflected the growing awareness within the United Nations system of the importance of participation as a development objective and of the need for concrete initiatives to strengthen the participatory imperative in the rural development activities of the different United Nations agencies.

The work programme of the Panel, drawn up at its meeting in January 1982, comprises conceptual, analytical work; exchange of experience among developing countries in participatory initiatives at the grass-roots level; reorientation of existing programmes to incorporate or strengthen participatory approaches; initiation of joint field projects; and mobilisation of resources for programmes and projects seeking to promote authentic participation by the rural poor. The present study represents an important element of the work programme of the Panel. It was felt that while there was a growing acceptance of participation as a development objective, reflected in part in increasing references to people's participation in official documents and debates on development, there was also a great deal of misunderstanding and confusion about its meaning and objectives and approaches to its promotion. Consequently, there was a need for a simple, coherent and succinct statement aimed at clarification of the diverse interpretations of the term, distillation of the experience with participatory approaches by different agencies, and provision of guidance on the future development of analytical and operational work on participation by the agencies.

The study by Peter Oakley and David Marsden goes a long way in fulfilling this difficult and challenging task. The authors have wisely eschewed the easy path of producing a manual containing a mechanical listing of definitions of participation, of obstacles to its promotion and of projects and programmes ostensibly designed to strengthen participatory aspects. Instead, they have sought in a subtle and sensitive manner to trace the roots of alternative interpretations of participation to fundamental differences in perceptions of the development process and to illustrate approaches to participation through sketches of concrete initiatives. They have also made a start with an analysis of the emerging elements of a strategy for participatory development.

The authors contrast two interpretations of participation: the one more widely accepted is to view participation as an input to development. The people are "mobilised" to implement activities generally decided by outsiders. This instrumental and interventionist interpretation is contrasted with the view which regards participation as "empowering" the rural poor to play an effective role in rural development. While recognising some attributes of the latter view of participation, the authors repeatedly stress the difficulty of catching its essence in a formal definition. An important feature of participation as "empowering the poor" is voluntary, spontaneous and often gradual growth of organised group activity, preceded by a process of collective reflection and characterised by active involvement of members and by self-reliance. The process is often but not always initiated by some outside activists. But it is quite impossible at this stage to generalise on the direction and mechanics of evolution of such groups.

Some indication of what is involved in this process is given in the five illustrative accounts of participatory processes presented in the study. These range from pressure-group activity, such as in Bhoomi Sena, to health improvement in Ecuador and include official attempts at participation promotion both at the local level, as in Nepal, and at the national level, as in Ethiopia. One illustration deals with the effort of fisherwomen in Brazil to organise and improve their living conditions. These case studies illustrate a wide diversity in initial objectives, the methods used to promote organisation and participation and the results achieved.

In the concluding chapter, the authors seek to draw together the common elements of a participatory approach to development. While recognising that there is no universal model of participation, they delineate some of the building blocks of a more complete analysis of the theory and practice of participatory approach to development. It is to be hoped that this study will stimulate further efforts to advance our understanding of this approach

through reflection on the myriad of participatory initiatives
under way in various parts of the Third World.

Dharam Ghai
Chairman
Panel on People's Participation

TABLE OF CONTENTS

Page

PREFACE... v

INTRODUCTION... 1

CHAPTER 1   THE CONTEXT OF PARTICIPATION..................... 5

    1.1 Development strategy....................... 5
    1.2 Re-think.................................. 7
    1.3 The rural poor............................ 10
    1.4 Participation as a strategy for
         rural development....................... 13

CHAPTER 2   THE CONCEPT OF PARTICIPATION..................... 17

    2.1 Introduction.............................. 17
    2.2 Interpretation............................ 18
    2.3 Implementation............................ 20

        2.3.1 Collaboration - input -
               sponsorship...................... 20
        2.3.2 Community development.............. 22
        2.3.3 Organisation...................... 23
        2.3.4 Empowering........................ 25

    2.4 Means or end.............................. 27
    2.5 Obstacles................................. 29
    2.6 Comment................................... 31

CHAPTER 3   THE PRACTICE OF PARTICIPATION................... 37

    3.1 Small farmers' development programme
         (SFDP) - Nepal......................... 39
    3.2 Participation in rural health............. 43
    3.3 Bhoomi Sena, India........................ 46
    3.4 Fisherwomen and participation,
         Brazil................................. 50
    3.5 The structure of national participation
         - Ethiopia............................. 54
    3.6 Comment................................... 58

CHAPTER 4   AN EMERGING STRATEGY............................ 63

    4.1 The basis of a strategy................... 63
    4.2 Approach.................................. 65
    4.3 Method.................................... 69

        4.3.1 Pedagogy.......................... 70
        4.3.2 Groups............................ 71
        4.3.3 Agent of participation............ 74

    4.4 Evaluation................................ 77
    4.5 Project activities........................ 78
    4.6 Comment................................... 80

CHAPTER 5   CONCLUDING STATEMENT............................ 81

"What gives real meaning to popular participation
is the collective effort by the people concerned
to pool their efforts and whatever other resources
they decide to pool together, to attain _objectives_
they set for themselves. In this regard participation is viewed as an _active process_ in which the
participants take initiatives and action that is
stimulated by their _own_ thinking and deliberation
and over which they _can_ exert effective _control_.
The idea of passive participation which _only_
involves the people in actions that have been
thought out or designed by others and are controlled
by others is unacceptable."

(ACC Task Force, Working Group on Programme
Harmonization, Rome, 1978)

* Our underlining *

exist, and which marginalise women, remain unquestioned. Women in rural areas face a layer of structural and cultural constraints which restrict and bias their participation. The establishment of joint organisations in strategies for change often means that their interests are re-submerged. No account is taken of the female-specific nature of many of the problems that women face, or of the different networks in which they interact, which produce a very different, but seldom appreciated, configuration of interests. While recognising this we felt that much more attention needed to be paid to the issue of the participation of rural women through a separate study. In this volume we have attempted to evaluate critically various approaches to participation in rural development rather than address ourselves to what might be seen as the particular problems of so-called "target groups".

It was also the original intention that this study should consider both the issues of <u>obstacles</u> and <u>approaches</u> to participation in rural development. On completing the first draft of the study, however, we realised that we had in fact addressed ourselves more directly to the issue of "approaches". The two issues, whilst inter-related, do demand separate treatment and we felt that it was impossible to give them equal treatment in one study. We noted also that work had already begun in terms of identifying "obstacles" to participation and we did not wish merely to duplicate such work. From the point of view of our own experiences, we felt that we could make a more positive contribution by concentrating our study on "approaches" to participation which is an area which has been less prominently examined. We do consider the issue of "obstacles" in our text but not to any great depth. Our primary concern has been to highlight the <u>ways</u> in which rural development projects are trying to bring about the participation of the rural poor.

Finally, it is quite possible to approach the concept of participation in rural development from a wide range of perspectives, (i.e. organisation and participation, obstacles to participation, etc.). Indeed our biggest headache has been how to give this study a coherent perspective, considering the all-embracing nature of the term "participation". This study, therefore, should be seen as a contribution to an ongoing inquiry and <u>not</u> a definitive statement. Given the concern of the United Nations agencies for the operationa-lisation of the concept and given the nature of the Panel, it was agreed therefore that our perspective would be <u>participation in</u>

<u>rural development programmes or projects</u>.   The majority of the
agencies represented on the Panel which commissioned this paper
employ the programme or project as their means of intervention in
rural development.   It was necessary to define quite narrowly the
perspective to be adopted, otherwise the study could have dealt
with anything and everything concerning participation.

We hope that a concentration on this particular <u>form</u> of intervention does not preclude an evaluation of the many "external"
pressures that impinge on programme/project design and implementation.   On the contrary we hope that our particular focus will
serve as an enabling device which enhances our ability to come to
terms with what is a very complex issue.   It is not possible, of
course, to isolate this level of intervention and overlook its
relationship with the wider socio-political structure.   Although,
therefore, our conceptualisation and discussion of participation
is broad-based, our detailed analysis of its practice is in the
context of project and programme intervention on rural development.

In the writing of this paper we managed briefly to discuss its
contents with a number of Panel members from ILO, FAO, WHO, IFAD and
UNRISD.   We are grateful to these colleagues for their assistance
and for the documentation which they inevitably supplied.   The task
has been undertaken with some haste and, inevitably in such circumstances, more time and a different time of the year would have given
us more satisfaction.   Equally inevitably, somebody will surely
comment that the preparation of this paper should have been a
"participatory" exercise.   But that may be the reality of all
participatory exercises!

Peter Oakley   David Marsden
March, 1983.

Chapter 1

THE CONTEXT OF PARTICIPATION

1.1 Development strategy

The present search for a new international economic and social
order reflects the build-up of a profound disillusionment with
established development strategies.   These latter emphasised
economic growth and industrialisation in the context of increasingly
centralised planning and control over the distribution of resources.
The orthodox ideas, encapsulated in what has come to be termed a
"modernisation" approach, stressed the injection of capital inputs
from outside which would result in "take off" and the eventual
spread of benefits throughout the system.   Newly emergent independent nations would be given a helping hand up the evolutionary ladder
that had already been climbed by those nations who had gone through
the stage of industrialisation.   Emphases were laid on providing
the infrastructural facilities and institutions to facilitate this
climb and on tackling the obstacles that were to be found on the
way.

In this context the rural poor within these developing countries
were not seen as the major resources for furthering the process of
development, but rather as obstacles, and attention was turned to
mobilising them through mass education and community development
programmes to reach the critical "take off" point into self-
sustained growth.   The rural areas were perceived to be lagging
behind the national development effort;   agriculture had to be
improved to support the industrialisation process.   Projects and
programmes designed to smooth the path were formulated by urban
administrators and planners and little attention was paid to the
rural populations who were regarded as traditional, even primitive,
and who, in a paternalistic way, needed to be educated out of their
ignorance.

Such strategies tended to ignore the growing cleavages in
society which the "benefits" of modernisation seemed to be producing.
There were massive dislocations of populations as a result of urban
migration and increasing evidence of growing inequalities as certain
sections of society seemed to be able to capture the benefits whilst
others, a growing majority, were excluded from them.   These
strategies were based on a rather one-sided view of society in which

it was assumed that people could and should live in harmonious
communities working for the benefit of the nation.

Public emphasis was placed on nation-building and on community
development. It was seldom acknowledged that such processes might
be being built upon social orders which were far from democratic
and that support was being given to maintain and entrench sometimes
very inegalitarian social systems, however inadvertently. In the
1970s the naïve and unreflexive certainties, which characterised
the enthusiasm of the 1950s, were beginning to be renegotiated as
the complexities of the development process were recognised and as
the faith in the Western industrialised nations' strategies was
called into question.

It became increasingly obvious that the officially endorsed
economic development policies and programmes were themselves part
of the problem. Early attempts to address this issue took the form
of an identification of the "social" dimensions of development. It
was felt that earlier failures were the result of a neglect of the
"human factor" and efforts were made to incorporate those who had
been marginalised by the development process into the national
drive and also to get rid of the obstacles to that process which
lay in the traditional attitudes of certain sectors of the population;
largely those who lived in outlying rural and tribal areas.

The techniques to be employed in the incorporation of the "human
factor" were seen to be akin to those employed by the economist.
But as the gap between proclaimed goals and reality seemed to widen
and the difficulties of actually measuring "social" development
became more obvious, the space for conceptual confusion increased
and the contradictions associated with these orthodox strategies
became more apparent.

While it **might** well be argued that development, measured in
primarily economic terms, has occurred and that participation has
increased, as more and more sectors of the population have been
incorporated into larger and more complex societies (the monetisa-
tion of economies has proceeded apace and markets for cash goods
are available virtually everywhere), it might be argued that this
incorporation was itself part of the problem. The new structures
that were emerging provided fewer opportunities for people's involvement, as the resources available seemed to accumulate in the hands
of fewer and fewer people. There was indeed a massive increase in

food production, for example, but the control of land by a smaller
group of people meant that the benefits of such increases did not
necessarily go to the actual producers.

1.2 Re-think

It is in this confused conceptual climate that a re-think of
development strategies is occurring. It is very difficult to
isolate the many inter-related elements that underpin this search
for an alternative approach to forms of action/intervention or to
chart a course through the mass of competing explanations, and show
how they are fundamentally different from those adopted in the past
and also how they have resulted in a re-alignment of interests
focused on a particular section of the national population - the
rural poor.

The search for more appropriate styles of development is fundamentally linked to what has been termed "dependency theory". This
reflects a shifting paradigm in which explanations of poverty are
seen in a new light, and represents a shift in the ways in which
questions are posed and solutions elaborated. It is associated
with the writings of people like Frank and Freire and has its
greatest elaboration in Latin American practice. But that is not
the only element in the changing equation. The "limits to growth"
debate highlighted the destructive nature of sophisticated technological progress and the effects of industrialisation on the environment and called for more ecologically sound development strategies.
The ideas associated with one particular global development path
were being replaced by calls for more appropriate strategies which
took into account the individuality of nations and regions. The
examples of China and of Tanzania stand out as models in this search
for appropriateness which became linked to strategies for endogenous
and self-reliant development.

The negative side-effects of industrialisation, the increasing
demands for employment and the satisfaction of basic needs, which
were not being met by capital-intensive growth strategies, served to
focus attention on the rural areas. The policies adopted unilater-
ally by those who had access to the instruments of power served to
focus attention on the problems of the disadvantaged and the
excluded who were to be found in a majority in the rural areas.

This search for a new order which emphasises the poor and the
rural areas is not new. It has its roots in reactions to early

forms of industrialisation in the West.   What is new is the
centrality that it has been afforded in international thinking in
recent years.   It focuses around the concepts of dependency and of
exploitation, both normative concepts which are very difficult to
define except in relation to particular historical circumstances.
It has its roots in a history of colonial expansion and a reinter-
pretation of that expansion.   Rather than being seen as a civilis-
ing process the colonial experience is reinterpreted as a history
of "subordination" and "exploitation" and as such has resulted in
a profound distrust for "outsiders" and in calls for autonomous
development strategies.

This historical experience has led to a thorough questioning
of the relationships between the dominant and the subordinate powers.
How far, for example, is the continuing poverty of these newly
independent countries linked to the former colonising powers? How
far is the industrialisation process dependent on maintaining that
poverty?   In other words, is active underdevelopment to be linked
directly to continuing relations of subordination?   While answers
to such questions must remain hypothetical, in that they cannot be
proved conclusively, they nevertheless provided an important new
focus whereby explanations of continued poverty might be addressed
with new conceptual tools.

"Dependency theory", if that is what one can call it, is
characterised by a marked pessimism about the possibilities for
development, particularly capitalist forms of development.   For it
is argued that such forms of development inevitably increase
dichotomies and engender the enrichment of a few at the expense of
the many: the obstacles to development are perceived to lie, not
in the "traditional" and "backward" nature of society, but in the
subordinate and marginalised role that countries have in the world
economy.   It is further argued that the ruling élites within these
countries have co-operated with international capital to obstruct
an independent development, and that they have encouraged an
"unbalanced" development in which attention is focused on capital-
intensive luxury consumer goods industries and unequal terms of
trade ensure that surpluses are transferred out of the country,
thereby stunting the development process.

Such an interpretation of the process of change does not
exclude an industrialisation strategy, but rather suggests an

approach which attempts to avoid the dependent associations with the international economy and, perhaps justifiably, an approach which focuses on agriculture and the rural areas as <u>spaces</u> where dependency might be most easily avoided. Furthermore attention has focused on the subordination of nations to other nations, as if they were themselves actors on the world stage. This has, by analogy, led to an appreciation of what has sometimes been called "internal colonisation", manifest in the subordination of particular regions to the capital city, of rural to urban areas, of poor people to rich patrons, of share-croppers to landowners and of women to men. The focus of subordination may vary greatly; the processes involved are the same.

This interpretation cuts across the wholistic arguments for a unified development based on the development of so-called "communities" which operate in the "national" interest and which assume that everyone is, or should be, pulling in the same direction. Rather, it enables people to identify particular groups with conflicting interests and points towards an alternative analysis of society in which different interest groups struggle for control of available assets and resources. It looks at the processes of impoverishment and enrichment which characterise existing relationships of inequality and sees both processes as obstacles to the development process. "Dependency theory" offers different conceptual tools for analysis, locating the international agencies and national governments within the context of the problem, alerting them to the complexities of the issues involved, as well as to their roles as active agents in the processes of development and underdevelopment. They are seen as part of the problem rather than as neutral arbiters in some idealistic and ahistorical universe.

It was in the 1970s that attempts to deal with this dilemma began to surface in the establishment debate and different types of alternative strategies were explored. These reacted to those who wished to link development with "liberation", seen as a way of enhancing the control of the disadvantaged over resources, and who maintained that effective development necessarily implied radical structural change. A major vehicle for the elaboration of alternatives has been the periodical <u>Development Dialogue</u>, published by the Dag Hammarskjöld Foundation, which has coined the term "another development". The development philosophy adopted is one which stresses the qualitative and perhaps unmeasurable dimensions of development; values which give a sense of fulfilment. Self-reliance is highlighted in the context of a participatory democracy in which the "consciousness-gap" between the leaders of society and the masses is closed and in which man is seen as the subject of his own world rather than the object of other people's worlds. Emphasis is placed on an empowering process which through organisation gives people the strength to create a space for themselves, and to build up material assets to support their own self-reliant development.

1.3 The rural poor

Such a philosophy holds the issue of participation as central and is primarily associated with the rural poor, not only because they are the most disadvantaged within society, but also because the rural areas in comparison with the urban areas, which constitute the industrial base, have been relatively neglected by previous development strategies. This philosophy of a "people-based" development "from below" assumes that participation is not only an end in itself but also a fundamental pre-condition for and a tool of any successful development strategy. The failure of past development strategies is fundamentally linked to the absence of this missing ingredient - participation.

But who are the rural poor? The category is extremely broad and does not necessarily allow us to differentiate between those who are being impoverished or enriched within such a category (if such a differentiation is indeed possible in terms of distinct human agents). The composition of the rural poor has been variously analysed.[1] A variety of other terms such as "underprivileged", "disadvantaged" and "low income groups", have also been used to describe the large majority of people in rural areas. Development projects have by and large failed to reach this section of the rural population. Benefits have often been "captured" by the rural élites. This seems to be particularly the case when one looks at the "male bias" in such projects which have largely presumed that, because women are parts of male-dominated households, their interests are reflected in the interests of their husbands or fathers.

Whilst no statement on the rural poor can have universal application and, indeed any normative statement might be regarded as aggregating competing interests in any specific context, the following encapsulates the major elements of our target group:

...that section of the rural population whose basic minimum needs for life, and existence with human dignity, are unfulfilled. Such a condition of poverty is characterised by low incomes, widely associated with various forms of oppression under social structures through which dominant social groups are able to dictate the conditions of life of the dominated and to appropriate much of the product of the latter's labour and often also the material assets the latter may initially possess.[2]

We are dealing therefore with the great mass of the people in rural areas: small farmers, tenants, share-croppers, the landless and also women. Women are often veiled behind these disadvantaged groups and thus forgotten in any formal categorisation, and in being disguised frequently suffer the harsher extremes of poverty. The rural poor are often geographically, socially and culturally isolated. They commonly lack the productive assets other than their labour power, which would enable them to struggle for independence. They remain attached in dependent ways to those who have control over land and capital.

A review of the literature would indicate the following as the kinds of problems which affect the rural poor's chances of improving the bases of their livelihood:

- lack of access to resources for development;
- lack of viable organisations to represent their interests;
- the dominant power of local moneylenders and traders;
- the dependent and marginalised nature of their lives;
- the air of despondency and despair which characterise their lives.

The literature is graphic on their plight and their poverty and despite "poverty-focused" programmes, a major obstacle has been in actually reaching the poorest of the poor. Some impact in terms of relief of a temporary nature seems to have been felt but, without major structural changes, the problem remains largely unaddressed. A radical reassessment of project design and implementation is called for to address these issues and these in turn require a radical change in the patterns and processes of intervention in the rural areas.

As indicated earlier, there is a major problem in focusing on the "rural poor" as a "target group". It is felt that this focus poses the danger of actually excluding from analysis those groups in society who might be responsible for the process of impoverishment. We need to be able to see both sides of the coin. To whom are we actually referring when we talk of the rural poor? Traditional rural development projects have identified specific sectors of the rural population and directed their attention to them. Co-operative development projects, for example, bring together male participants with minimum access to land. Small farmers' development programmes focus on just that group. By implication the others who live with the co-operators or small farmers are excluded. The thinking behind the isolation of particular sectors would appear to be largely an elaboration of an ideology which emphasises the identification and stimulation of individual entrepreneurs. It was perhaps assumed that such persons represented the interests of the village or the "community" and that to focus on them would result in the "trickle-down" of benefits. While this was the case in some instances, it also had the effect of excluding others and perpetuating and enhancing divisions within the village.

Alternative development strategies break quite decisively with this perception of the community as some sort of concensual unity, and attempt to identify and work with distinct socio-economic groups with common interests that perhaps run counter to the interests of the established, visible élites in the community. These strategies are specifically aimed at the non-visible and those without voices. Under such circumstances the chances of hitting an invisible target are slender. There may be no cohesion in the "group" identified and thus one of the major aims is actually to remove the veil which hides them and be involved in the pre-history of other organisation. The literature on the composition of such groups, while increasing, remains scanty because of the problems of visibility. Their size, structure and purposes vary greatly according to the particular environment in which they are found and the pre-history of their establishment. They operate in a complex environment in which relationships are rapidly changing and in which their organisation is both cause and effect of that change in the negotiation of a new order and in their participation in the benefits of that changing order. The obstacles to their emergence, perpetration and growth are located in the old order which is giving birth to them and their demands for participation take on new dimensions as they grow. Their growth is stimulated and to some extent legitimated with help from outsiders who can create the space for their growth.

When we talk of the "rural poor", therefore, it is impossible to conceptualise them as a static, homogeneous group which can be

readily identified and moulded.   They are a dynamic and fragmented
population and one of the aims of isolating them is to increase
their awareness of a whole series of common interests which might
give them the strength and the opportunity to organise.   It is
increasingly important to understand the existence of discrete
common interest groups and the complex web of relationships between
them.   Their increased participation is essential for the elaboration of the new order because on their participation rests the future
of all development initiatives.

1.4 Participation as a strategy
for rural development

Most people would agree that increased participation is a
"good" thing.   It is put centre-stage now because it is seen as
strategically important.   But the tactics that one adopts to implement this strategy will vary according to the point of view that one
adopts about the role/nature of rural intervention.   One can, at
the risk of grotesquely oversimplifying, identify two types of
strategy.   First, there is that which is based on the assumption
that there is little wrong with the direction of the development
effort and that past failures are largely because the "human factor"
has been neglected and people have not wanted to get involved in
projects about which they had little information or they were dubious.
Such assumptions lead to the elaboration of extension strategies
which are meant to "fill the gap", inject more information, increase
the knowledge base.   If the people are involved, they will commit
themselves to the support of projects.

Secondly, as a result of the re-think in development strategies,
there is that strategy which assumes that the direction of the
development effort is fundamentally misconceived.   Here, participation is seen as a strategy for the creation of opportunities to
explore new, often open-ended directions with those who were tradi-
tionally the objects of development.   The tactics involved in such
a strategy are fundamentally different.   More knowledge may not be
required; it is rather the knowledge of the rural poor that has not
been incorporated.   It is not the failure to take into account the
"human factor" which is at fault, but rather the unreflexive way
in which the developers were left out of the equation and the rather
unilateral way in which they dealt with what were regarded as passive
recipients - consumers rather than producers.   Participation in

this sense is concerned therefore with the production of knowledge, new directions, new modes of organisation rather than with the dissemination of more of the same.

Whatever assumptions one operates with, ideas about participation converge in a concern for giving the rural poor a voice in development decisions, access to productive assets and a share in development. Participation is a multi-dimensional process which varies from location to location in response to particular circumstances. There is no one way of looking at it and its interpretation is very much a function of the analysis employed.

Given the convergence of emphases on this process, there have been a whole host of attempts to engender, operationalise and extend the participation of the poor in rural development. Participation is a major concern for United Nations agencies such as the ILO, WHO, FAO, IFAD and UNESCO. Some have set up particular bodies to explore its dimensions and UNRISD has devoted a major branch of its research work to a popular participation programme. In 1976 the ILO-sponsored World Employment Conference (WEC) identified the issue of "basic needs" and the crucial role of participation in such a strategy. Its PORP (Participatory organisations of the Rural Poor) programme was launched in 1977 and has already produced a number of informative studies. Also the ILO's assistance to rural workers' organisations and support for workers' educational activities to bring about effective participation have been important programmes for many years. In 1978 the WHO-sponsored Alma-Ata Conference similarly stressed the importance of "participation" in extending primary health care and providing health for all by the year 2000. In 1979 the WCARRD's declaration of principles and programme of action stress the fundamental importance of participation in rural development. This has led to the FAO-sponsored People's Participation Programme (PPP) which seeks to promote rural development on the principle of effective participation. Participation is an important and growing element in IFAD's rural credit projects. Similarly, following the 1978 conference on Participation in Rural Development organised by UNESCO in Lima, Peru, research carried out in the Caribbean and in Africa on small farmers and food crops, has closely meshed with action encouraging small farmers to participate in rural development policies and decisions through organisation. Outside the United Nations system the promotion of participation has become a major plank of the activities of non-governmental organisations (NGOs) in their shift from relief and improvement efforts to the

support of efforts to tackle what are perceived to be more fundamental problems of lack of access, assets and voice.   This NGO
concern is illustrated, for example, by the World Council of
Churches' Commission on the Church's Participation in Development.

In the past decade, and particularly since the WEC in 1976,
a large amount of resources has gone into the promotion of participation.   The results of this investment, however, are still unclear.
Before we examine the varied practice to date, it would be useful
to analyse the concept of participation and see what it means to
those who employ it in the context of rural development.

Notes:

[1] P. Devitt: "Notes on poverty-orientated rural development",
in Extension, planning and the poor (London, ODI, 1977); S.D. Briggs:
The rural poor: Obstacles which prevent the development of agri-
cultural technologies for their benefit (New Delhi, CIMMYT, 1979);
ILO: Poverty and landlessness in rural Asia (Geneva, 1977);
G. Hunter: Agricultural development and the rural poor (London,
ODI, 1978); FAO: Research guidelines for field action projects
(Rome, ROAP, 1979).

[2] Md. A. Rahman: "Concept of an inquiry", in Development:
Seeds of change (Rome, SID), 1981, No. 1, p. 3.

Chapter 2

THE CONCEPT OF PARTICIPATION

2.1 Introduction

As we have seen in Chapter 1, it is impossible to disentangle
the concept of participation from some understanding of rural
development.   Indeed in the past decade it has come to be heralded
by some as a key element in rural development; if only it could be
meaningfully inserted into the "development process", success would
be ensured.   Much of the literature on participation sees participation as the "missing ingredient" in this development process; a
tangible input which can be physically inserted into rural development projects.[1]   Yet few references to the concept present any
analysis of its fundamental nature or consider the substantial
implications of implementation.

Popular participation has been conceptualised in relation to
some form of political democracy and, equally broadly, in terms of
involvement in the processes of societal change and growth that the
term "development" suggests.[2]   More commonly in development literature it is examined from the point of view of government intervention in development, and in this respect, terms such as "mobilisation" and "coercion" have been used to characterise the nature of
the "participation".   The "intervention" is itself conceptualised
into some kind of planning process with the accompanying paraphernalia
of mechanisms, objectives, budgets and control.   It is true to say
that the more commonly conceptualised understanding of "participation"
in rural development is presented in the context of that apparatus.
Participation is in fact perceived as a kind of injcotion which can
be applied to a rural development project and consequently help
influence its outcome.

Conversely, where "participation" emerges as a result of some
kind of bottom-up process, it is characterised as being "authentic"
and focusing on distribution.   Whilst some would disagree it is
hard not to associate this latter form of "participation" more
directly with the non-government sector.   In this understanding of
"participation" the emphasis is upon education and the building up
of the organisational basis with which certain groups within the
rural sector might achieve their participation.   Implicit also is
some form of consciousness-raising and preparation for the task of
participating.

Participation is, however, generally understood as a <u>process</u>
and not as some kind of static end product of development.   And
yet when the dimension of <u>time</u> is introduced the positions diverge;
one school would argue that "participation" can be manipulated
within the context of the time of a particular intervention;   whilst
others argue the unpredictable nature of authentic "participation".
The concept of time in terms of a process of participation is, of
course, related to the task to be undertaken, which itself is a
function of the development perspective employed.   This process
has also been conceptualised in terms of discrete stages (marginal/
substantial/structural participation) although a major difficulty
arises concerning the understanding of the content of each stage.[3]
Similarly where typologies of "participation" are discussed, such
terms as "spontaneous", "induced" or "coerced" are used.[4]

In the context of rural development we are not concerned in
the first instance with how to achieve a totally participatory
society.   We are more concerned with how to bring about some
meaningful involvement in the development of the rural sector on
the part of those who depend on that sector for a livelihood.   It
is common knowledge that the benefits of this development have been
unevenly distributed over the past two decades;   "participation"
is suggested as the means by which this trend might be reversed.
"Participation" is seen as the means for a widening and redistribution of opportunities to take part in societal decision-making, in
contributing to development and in benefiting from its fruits.

2.2   Interpretation

Although there is unanimity on the importance of "participation"
to achieve the desired redistribution of the benefits of development,
there is less unanimity on the nature and content of the "participation" process.   One of the most obvious features of the literature
explaining "participation", is the wide range of statements presented.   Some statements go little beyond public rhetoric;   that
is, they explain "participation" in supposedly neutral ways and such
unrealistic terms as to make it meaningless.[5]   In others a wide
range of ambiguous terms such as "self-help", "self-reliance",
"community involvement", "co-operation", "decentralisation" and
"local-level autonomy" add to the air of generalisation.

We would agree with several authors who have argued that it is
impossible to establish a universal definition of "participation".

As the UNRISD study points out, even with a working definition it
is impossible to identify "participation" as an "actual social
reality".[6]   Rahman even argues that, given its complex "nature",
"participation" can be explored but not contained in a formal
definition.[7]   However, working statements or interpretations are
necessary if the process is to be understood at all and, in this
respect, most documents or project reports present us with some kind
of working statement.   It is instructive to review the major ones
here.   We present them as though on a continuum (the limits of
which reflect the divergent perspectives outlined in Chapter 1) in
order to emphasise the conflicting range of interpretations which
themselves reflect the dominant paradigms of development thinking:

(a)   Participation is considered a voluntary contribution by
the people to one or another of the public programmes
supposed to contribute to national development but the
people are not expected to take part in shaping the
programme or criticising its content.[8]

(b)   Participation means ... in its broadest sense, to sensitise
people and, thus, to increase the receptivity and ability
of rural people to respond to development programmes, as
well as to encourage local initiatives.[9]

(c)   With regard to rural development ... participation includes people's involvement in decision-making processes,
in implementing programmes ... their sharing in the
benefits of development programmes, and their involvement
in efforts to evaluate such programmes.[10]

(d)   Popular participation in development should be broadly
understood as the active involvement of people in the
decision-making process in so far as it affects them.[11]

(e)   Community involvement means that people, who have both the
right and the duty to participate in solving their own
health problems, have greater responsibilities in assessing
the health needs, mobilising local resources and suggesting new solutions, as well as creating and maintaining
local organisations.[12]

(f)   Participation is considered to be an active process,
meaning that the person or group in question takes
initiatives and asserts his/her or its autonomy to do so.[13]

(g)   ... the organised efforts to increase control over
resources and regulative institutions in given
social situations, on the part of groups and movements
of those hitherto excluded from such control.[14]

The interpretations above move from the general to the more
specific.   Based on our review of project literature, we suggest
that statements (a), (b) and (c) reflect the dominant paradigm and
indeed the more commonly expressed understanding of participation.

Statements (d) and (e) can be seen in contrast to the previous
statements but are dominated by terms that themselves demand explanation, i.e. decision-making/greater responsibilities. Statements
(f) and (g) reflect the emerging rural development re-think of the
mid-1970s and inextricably equate participation with the achieving
of some kind of power. The first statements have a brisk, no-
nonsense and businesslike tone about them, reflecting the project or
programme nature of participation with the built-in specific
objectives and procedures. The latter statements illustrate more
meaningfully the process nature of participation, emphasise the
fact of group participation and highlight more dramatically the
essentially active nature of participation. All the statements are
predicated upon the particular perspective of rural development
being employed.

2.3 Implementation

A review of the literature reveals a wide range of key terms
or expressions which essentially characterise the nature of the
participation in reference. Indeed in our discussions with agency
representatives we attempted to sum up agency's interpretations of
participation in these key terms. Such an exercise helps to
encapsulate what is often a very diffuse explanation and practice
and also highlights the conflicting fundamental objectives of the
participation process. The terms themselves are not all self-
explanatory and they do not fit into any obvious typology. Given,
however, the emphasis of this paper with rural development and its
implementation, we have decided to present the terms in four broad
categories.

2.3.1 Collaboration - input -
sponsorship

The understanding of participation in these three terms is
inherent in statements (a), (b) and (c) above. Whilst these terms
demand more specific definition, they all reflect a form of participation in which government is the chief protagonist. Indeed it could
be argued that in this form "participation" equals "informing" and
that the basic decisions concerning development have already been
taken. This school of thought is unable to disassociate "participation" from government responsibility and control.

In its broadest sense this form of "participation" can be
equated with mobilisation. Mobilisation is an important dynamic

in development practice and reflects both an underlying ideology which argues the need to mobilise the rural sector in order to transform it and make it more "modern" and "responsive" and also the practice of mobilising rural labour for capital formation and in order to relieve scarce government resources. Essentially, therefore, in this form of "participation" the basic decisions which underlie the development action have already been taken and government bureaucracy, in the process of implementation, invites the rural population to endorse and to collaborate with the decisions taken.

In this situation it becomes increasingly difficult to understand the application of, for example, statement (c). A whole genre of "participation" literature deals with the rural populations' supposed participation in decision-making, implementation, benefits and the evaluation of the development action. A similar genre offers a body of prescriptions which argues the need for governments to, i.e.:

- bring about effective decentralisation in order to facilitate local decision-making,
- introduce effective co-ordination at the local level in order to promote local participation,
- and establish local level planning mechanisms in which the people can effectively participate.[15]

Given the radical structural and bureaucratic modifications which would be required to bring about such changes, it can be seen that the presentation of participation in these terms is quite unrealistic. There are few examples of rural people effectively participating in "the planning process".[16] Similarly, if we consider the following normative statement on the decision-making process in the context of rural development, viz.:

Decision-making ... is taken as a broad process encompassing all the aspects of learning and research, analysis and debate which preface and influence the formal choice of policy or action.[17]

we can understand the radical changes to existing bureaucratic structures and planning procedures that would be required in order for such a statement to be implemented.

The overwhelming impression of this form of "participation" is that where it exists, it is on predetermined terms and reflected formally in participation in the process of production or in established legal institutions. Much of the literature in this respect refers to ideal states and inexplicably underestimates the profound consequences of participation in "decision-making" and "planning". In this form of participation the groundrules are previously established, participation is conceived as a manageable input, but the overwhelming majority of rural people remain excluded from any informed or systematic involvement in the events that affect their livelihood. It is essentially a _passive_ form of participation.

2.3.2 Community development

In some situations it is possible to get a more meaningful understanding of participation in rural development. This is the case when we examine certain specific types of rural development programmes i.e. health, water or physical infrastructure. In these instances the literature does not exaggerate the nature of the participation concerned, but demonstrates quite explicitly its limits. The participation is limited to the task at hand and it would appear that in these tasks the rural people _do_ have some kind of say. The participation involved is not institutionalised (unless some organisation form results) and, although the basic decisions regarding the task (i.e. national health priorities) have probably been taken, there is some meaningful discussion on interpretation and implementation. Much of the practice and experience of participation in this form can be found in case studies of community development.

The field of health is one in which the _active_ involvement of the rural population seems most to have been achieved. In this respect the following statement is illustrative:

> Community participation has been described as the process by which individuals, families or communities assume responsibility for their own health and welfare and develop the capacity to contribute to their own and the community's development.[18]

This participation is _actively_ promoted and involves some delegation of responsibility at the community level and the creation of local councils as vehicles of this participation.[19] The provision and management of water supply are also examples where local people can meaningfully participate. Indeed such participation is critical to the continuation of the water supply since external assistance invariably cannot be maintained.[20] Finally there is the substantial area of food aid, and the use of surplus food to generate capital improvements. There is, in fact, much debate on this controversial issue. Some would argue that the food acts as a catalyst or

stimulus to community participation and that the people do have some
meaningful say in the tasks undertaken.   Furthermore the experience
gained is useful for future community participation.   Others,
however, among other points, point to the dependency that food aid
can create and doubt the evidence of meaningful participation where
food is offered as an incentive to participate in food for work
programmes.

Undoubtedly in this type of community development, the voice
of the people is to some extent heard.   Unlike the more centrally
dominated agricultural policy, it would appear that in local efforts
to improve health and water, for example, local opinions and needs
are taken into account.   But the participation is confined to the
task at hand and there is little evidence that the experience is
used in order that the rural poor can tackle their more fundamental
problems.

2.3.3 Organisation

There is a strong body of thought in the literature which
argues that, if only the rural poor can be brought into some form
of organisational structure, their participation would be ensured.
Indeed this is the general tenor of the WCARRD whose declarations
are based on the assumption that "... active participation of the
poor can only be brought about by adequate people's organisations
at the local level".   Indeed some have gone so far as to define
participation in terms of a process by which the rural poor can
organise themselves and, through their own organisation, are able
to have some say in local development efforts.[21]   Inevitably linked
with the suggestion of rural organisation is the assumption that,
once such organisations are established, the "people" will auto-
matically have a voice and can influence decision-making.   The
organisation of the rural population is not a new phenomenon in
rural development.   Indeed formal organisational structures, i.e.
co-operatives and rural unions, were among the first structural
imports into the rural areas of the Third World.   Undoubtedly
formal organisations such as co-operatives did facilitate the participation of some in rural development and similarly brought tangible
economic benefits.   There is equally no doubt that such formal
organisations have been inadequate in facilitating the participation
of the rural poor.   The recent FAO ROAP study has confirmed this
and also illustrated how such organisations can lead to the further
impoverishment of the rural poor.[22]   This failure is not a

reflection on, for example, the co-operative institution per se but more on the bureaucratic constraints which limit the successful functioning of such institutions.

The search has begun, therefore, for authentic people's organisations which, if they can be conceived, will supposedly result in more meaningful participation and give those previously excluded access to development. This search appears to be directed in two different, but not mutually exclusive, ways:

    (a) those who seek to learn from the lessons of the past and propose reformed kinds of formal organisations within the existing socio-political framework;[23]

    (b) those who have no prescribed model, but who stress that such organisations must emerge as a result of the people's own deliberations.[24]

The first approach would appear to be predominant. This approach often calls upon governments to make meaningful reforms (i.e. "delegation of power and self-management to the rural people" and "democratic processes in all decision-making"),[25] in order to promote the emergence of people's organisations. It is within this climate in fact that the United Nations agencies have to cope with their re-examination of participation. Realistically it is difficult to imagine that a totally new climate will materialise which will right the wrongs of the past. Undoubtedly in this approach some rural people have participated effectively and gained tangible benefits. The approach, however, has not led to the meaningful participation of the rural poor in general.

The second approach is still very much in its infancy and there are as yet few substantial examples. This approach similarly draws upon the experience of the past but seeks a more radical prescription. There are some studies within the existing development bureaucracy which seek to determine a more authentic organisation for the rural people, and some of this research is also being done, in an unsystematic manner, by the non-governmental agencies.[26] This approach fundamentally seeks to avoid the introduction from outside of an organisational form but instead is researching the conditions under which an authentic form of organisation might meaningfully emerge from within the rural poor.[27] In other words, the creation of the organisation is part of the participation process. Organisation means strength and strength is a prerequisite to taking action. This process is closely linked to the Freirian type praxis and it is a process in which a crucial element concerns the nature and the role of the external intervention.

The relationship between organisation and participation is incontestable; it is the nature of the participation which is in debate. Where organisational forms are introduced from outside, the constraints upon meaningful participation are self-evident. Where an organisational form is to emerge as a result of a process of participation, however laudatory, it is equally self-evident the enormous pressures such a process will have to confront. It is improbable in the short term that such efforts will enjoy the protective cover of International Labour Convention No. 141 (1975) which seeks to establish the democratic right of rural workers to organise for their own ends. It is too early to be able to state with any confidence what form such authentic organisations should take and what exactly is involved in their emergency. Clearly, if it is to be meaningful, the process will confront the hostility of established national and local structures. The overwhelming commitment is still towards the introduction of organisation from outside. It is a formidable task in itself to re-examine this dominant practice. Established bureaucracies are not going suddenly to democratise existing structures and permit meaningful participation, WCARRD notwithstanding.[28] The search for an authentic organisational form to facilitate this meaningful participation is under way although this search has yet to be substantially reflected in the available literature.

2.3.4 Empowering

Until quite recently the above interpretations of "participation" have dominated the literature. Since then, and as a reflection of the rural development re-think which we referred to in Chapter 1, an explanation of "participation" as a process of empowering has begun to emerge. The more common interpretation equates "participation" with achieving <u>power</u>: that is power in terms of access to, and control of, the resources necessary to protect livelihood. The following are a number of statements illustrative of this understanding of "participation":

(a) ... the promotion of popular participation implies a redistribution of power (basically a conflictual process) and this calls for a scientific analysis which gives due recognition to political factors, social forces and the role of class in historical processes of social change.[29]

(b) ... participation is concerned with the distribution of power in society, for it is power which enables groups to determine which needs, and whose needs, will be met through the distribution of resources.[30]

(c)   ... power is the central theme of participation and ...
      participatory social action entails widely shared,
      collective power by those who are considered beneficiaries.
      The people become agents of social action and the power
      differentials between those who control and need
      resources is reduced through participation.[31]

It would appear that, although there is strong evidence in the
non-conventional literature of NGOs that the achieving "power" as
a fundamental prerequisite to the rural people meaningfully
participating in development has been already clearly recognised,
it has been the recent research sponsored by UNRISD which has
brought the issue to wider prominence.   This understanding of
"participation" contains three main elements:

- the sharing of power and of scarce resources;
- deliberate efforts by social groups to control their own
  destinies and improve their living conditions;
- opening up opportunities "from below".

The process in fact generates "countervailing" power to confront the
already well-established power configuration within any particular
context.   This process is also characterised as "creating space",
or the imperceptible movement of pushing out the frontiers and of
achieving space within which groups might begin to function and to
take action.   In another sense this process is linked more tangibly
to the creation of <u>assets</u>; that is the building up of a minimal
economic base for previously excluded groups in order to help them
achieve the means to intervene more powerfully in the development
process.   The interpretation of participation in terms of achieving
some kind of political or economic strength is evident in much of
the recent literature on the concept, both within the United Nations
system and outside.   It is now even widespreadly <u>implicit</u> in much
of what is written on "participation".   Wherever this literature
links the process of "participation" with "structural change" or
"redistribution of basic common assets", it is impossible to exclude
the achieving of "power" as the fundamental prerequisite for these
changes.   "Participation" to bring about structural change implies
the taking of <u>action</u>, and this action can only be taken from a
position of power.

The inquiry into "participation" and power is still in its
infancy and, apart from one or two well researched examples,[32] we
have little substantial knowledge upon the process involved.
However, it would appear that there are three main elements which
have so far emerged:

- the identification and structuring of discrete socio-economic
  groups as the basic social unit;
- a process of non-formal education and consciousness raising;
- some form of outside assistance which is instrumental in
  initiating and accompanying the process of empowering.

We shall examine these three issues in more detail later.
Suffice here to emphasise the increasing awareness and acceptance
that "participation" is indeed concerned with power. The development literature is overburdened with the documenting of previous
"participation" strategies, most of which it is accepted have
failed in terms of giving the majority of rural people any meaningful say in those issues which affect their livelihood. The concept
of "participation" as empowering is a radical departure from years
of more traditional practice. Although its conceptualisation is
simple and its argument difficult to refute, it is correct to say
that it both faces formidable barriers and that it is also difficult
to imagine governments and locally established structures offering
other than powerful opposition. Historically participation has
rarely been willingly conceded to previously excluded groups and
the encounter between opposing forces is the inevitable result.

2.4 Means or end

A broad distinction can be drawn in the vast amount of literature and the practice of "participation" between "participation" as
a means or as an end. Where "participation" is interpreted basically as a means it is essentially describing a state or an input
into a development programme; where it is interpreted as an end in
itself, it refers to a process the outcome of which is meaningful
participation. There is controversy, of course, as to whether
"participation" as means or end is compatible or whether there can
be any unity between them. It is a fundamental distinction and
one which has enormous implications for the nature of "participation" and the approaches adopted for its achievement.

Until recently, and either implicitly or explicitly, the notion
of "participation" as a means has dominated development practice.
The two main vehicles for implementing this notion of "participation" were:

(a) community development programmes which were aimed at "preparing"
     the rural population to collaborate with government develop-
     ment plans; and

(b)   the establishing of <u>formal organisations</u> (co-operatives,
      farmers' associations, etc.) which were to provide the
      structure through which the rural people could have some
      contact with and voice in development programmes.

There can be no doubt that considerable "economic" development was
achieved as a result of the above strategy but the evidence suggests
that only the few achieved any meaningful participation by this
means.   This strategy has <u>not</u> resulted in meaningful participation,
in any sense of the term, of the poor in rural development.   In
fact it is a strategy which has resulted in where we are today:
confronting the issue of the lack of meaningful participation in
rural development.

Participation as an end is the inexorable consequence of the
process of empowering and liberation.   The state of achieving
power and of meaningfully participating in the development process
is in fact the objective of the exercise.   There is no necessary
notion of fixed quantifiable development goals, although these often
accompany the process, but the major effort is concentrated upon
the empowering process.   One NGO in Latin America described the
objective of its work in this field as follows:

> The creation of groups able to diagnose and analyse their own
> problems, to decide upon collective action and to carry out
> such action to deal with these problems, <u>independent of out-
> side direction</u>.

Participation in the above sense is not easy to perceive.   The end
itself becomes difficult to define in precise terms since it is
related to the qualitative processes of achieving power and the
resulting ability to take independent action.   Because of its
unsubstantial nature, it is difficult to characterise and to witness.
It essentially occurs over time, and only prolonged observation can
help in its understanding.   At this moment much of the experience
to date of this form of participation is confined to project files
and field notes and we have little knowledge of its method.   It
does not lend itself to the bureaucratic inquiries of administrative
frameworks nor, to some extent, to established methods of social
research.   Yet although the evidence suggests that its practice is
becoming widespread, our knowledge of it remains unsystematic.

It has been suggested that the unity of participation as both
means and end is implicit in a number of national development
efforts, i.e. Tanzania, Viet Nam and Ethiopia.[33]   Elsewhere the

contradiction remains. Ideally "participation" should incorporate both extremes, but it is difficult to see how these extremes can be reconciled. Where "participation" is the means to achieving previously established development objectives, its strategy is to reform and improve. Where "participation" aims at achieving power in order to demand meaningful participation, it implicitly demands some kind of structural change. Both positions reflect different ideological perspectives. In these circumstances it seems improbable that the divergence can be reconciled.

2.5 Obstacles

There are few who could argue with the following statement:

> ... in spite of insistence on popular participation in
> United Nations development programmes, an examination of
> the performance is not encouraging. ... authentic popular
> participation seldom occurs.[34]

Similarly the FAO ROAP study concluded that organisations which have been established have not in fact led to the participation by the majority of the rural population.[35] There is no shortage of comment in the literature or analysis as to why "participation" has not been achieved. Some dismiss out of hand the very suggestion that there has even been a genuine commitment to participation:

> Even those governments who talk about people's participation
> want such participation on their own terms. They specify
> all the rules of the game, neutralise or co-opt all genuine
> people's organisations and reduce the concept of participa-
> tion to a farce.[36]

The majority of commentators, however, have tried to explain the causes of the lack of "participation" and, more tangibly, the obstacles which impede its implementation. Inevitably such explanations reflect the ideological paradigm employed by the commentator. In the next chapter we shall examine obstacles in the context of several specific case studies. Here we shall limit ourselves to a general review of the issue.

The identification of obstacles is, therefore, directly related to one's perspective on "participation". In this respect the "means" or "end" dichotomy is illustrative. To view "participation" as a means suggests a set of obstacles usually associated with the operational procedures of the task undertaken. On the other hand, to view "participation" as an end suggests obstacles which are more associated with structural and institutional relationships both at the national and local level. There is no lack of comment on the obstacles to "participation" with which most readers will be familiar. There seems little point, therefore, in reproducing them at length here.[37] We shall limit ourselves to reviewing the major areas of obstacles which commentators suggest, although such areas are not mutually exclusive:

(i) Operational: In view of the dominance of the understanding of "participation" as a "means" and of its relationship with development programmes, obstacles are identified in terms of the operational mechanism of the development programme. In this respect the Cornell study has become something of a Bible for those who wish to understand the obstacles to "participation" at the development project level.[38] The obstacles (or factors) more commonly referred to include over-centralised planning, inadequate delivery mechanisms, lack of local co-ordination, inappropriateness of project technology, irrelevant project content, lack of local structures and so on. These obstacles in fact refer not only to participation but, to a large extent, are the maladies of many rural development projects. In this respect it is difficult to isolate the obstacles particular to participation. One could go so far as to say that these obstacles have very little to do with "participation". These obstacles represent the instruments of an approach which packages a product and then invites collaboration and presents this as "participation". Whilst the issues referred to are genuine and very common difficulties which most rural development projects confront, it is very difficult to feel that these issues can be managed locally and manipulated in a way favourable to meaningful participation.

(ii) Cultural: Our understanding and sensitivity towards the cultural obstacles which constrain rural people from participation has grown in recent years. Previously the literature explained people's attitude towards "participation" largely in terms of the supposed "resistance to change". Writers such as Freire, however, took us emphatically into the people's world and introduced us to such concepts as "marginalisation", "dependence", and "oppression". For these commentators the rural masses constituted the "culture of silence" with no access to, voice or participation in, development. This analysis spawned a whole new genre of explanation as to why rural people do not participate in rural development programmes.

It is only quite recently, therefore, that development workers
have become sensitive to the accumulation of pressure and historical
tradition which overwnelms most rural people and constrains their
willing "participation".   Hunter's recent study admirably highlights the inherent weakness of most rural people, their fears of
opposition and their weariness to outside cajoling to get involved.[39]
The rural poor understand the constraints upon their own effective
action and, as experience in Latin America has shown, it is a daunting task to encourage the rural people to take the initiative and
seek participation.

(iii) Structural: Both (i) and (ii) above are inextricably tied
up with the structural support or opposition they receive.   These
structural obstacles, local, national and international, dictate the
climate in which participation can occur.   It is in this area of
structural constraints that much of the UNRISD study is located.[40]
It is a fact that in most countries the dominant relations of power
and production and the ideological values legitimising them constitute powerful structural obstacles to the promotion of popular
participation.   In UNRISD's terms these are the structures and
ideologies of "anti-participation" since they help perpetuate
grossly unequal access to and control over societal wealth and power.
It is argued that the persistence of these "anti-participatory"
structures has caused the failure of many local level initiatives
to promote participation.

These structural obstacles are fundamental to achieving participation and it is erroneous to think otherwise.   The structure
disseminates to the regional and local level and pervades all forms
of formal and informal institutions and relationships.   The
structure dictates the terms of participation and reacts oppressively
if those terms are redefined; its aim is to keep the rural people
in their place, as labour power and possibly as consumers.   Participation initiatives emanating from below, therefore, are faced with
the dilemma of attempting to flourish within the context of the
existing structure or of seeking positively to influence the
structure.   Much participation field endeavour takes the former
course and pushes at the frontiers; others challenge the structure
and are correspondingly dealt with.

2.6 Comment

The purpose of this chapter has been to examine conceptually
the varied dimensions of participation.   Such a task is important

if only to stress that the concept _is_ multi-dimensional and is
unable to be presented in any singular form. Similarly the link
between development analysis and participation has been emphasised,
thus, it is hoped, illustrating to those still in doubt that the
act of participation is not neutral. Just as all intervention in
rural development is predicated on a particular perception of
development, so statements on participation reflect the ideological
paradigm being used. It is simply not possible to consider participation as some kind of quantifiable ingredient to be injected into
a development project. It is essentially a qualitative process
which, if it is to be meaningful, implies some fundamental shifts
in thinking and action.

As such, therefore, it is impossible to present a universal
list of those factors which constrain this process. Any discussion
on obstacles must be related to the particular interpretation of
participation adopted. In this sense, we shall examine a number
of case studies in the next chapter and note the factors which
affect their differing approaches to participation. It would be
possible to examine one or more of the different interpretations and
suggest the main areas of such constraints, as has already been
done in the literature.[41] It is difficult to avoid the conclusion,
however, that the overriding obstacle to meaningful participation
by the rural poor in the development process lies with the prevailing
socio-political structure. It is folly to ignore this fact, as it
is to propose prescriptions which imply changes in the structure
which are unrealistic. The dominant paradigm of development
thinking is a powerful influence on development practice and
severely constrains the consideration of radical alternatives.

Yet it is important to learn from practice. After the widespread influence of the community development approach in the 1950s
and 1960s and since the mid-1970s, there has been an increasing
number of rural development projects which have consciously, in one
form or another, sought to promote participation. The practice has
been undertaken by government-sponsored projects as well as by a
highly diversified network of NGOs. Participation is a live,
dynamic process and thus there is a limit to the amount we can learn
merely from its conceptualisation. We shall now, therefore, examine
a number of examples of its practice which reflect the range of
interpretations of participation and which may help us to give the
concept more form and meaning.

Notes:

[1] See for example, Marshall Wolfe: Popular participation in development: Conceptual framework, New York, (United Nations, Department of Technical Co-operation for Development), 1982, paper prepared for the International Seminar on Popular Participation, Ljubljana, 17-25 May 1982, for a discussion of participation in these terms.

[2] A. Pearse and M. Stiefel: Inquiry into participation: A research approach (Geneva, UNRISD, 1979). Pearse and Stiefel discuss this understanding of participation in terms of a "process of incorporation".

[3] J. Migdal: Peasants, politics and revolution (Princeton University Press, 1974, pp. 237-252); also I. Askew: Assessment of local participation techniques in the provision of fertility regulating services (University of Exeter, Institute of Population Studies, 1982).

[4] United Nations: Popular participation as a strategy for promoting community level action and national development, New York, (United Nations, Department of International Economic and Social Affairs, 1981).

[5] Many statements on "participation" deal with complex issues in very generalised terms. A common example of this is the frequent reference to "decentralisation" as critical to a process of participation. Such references rarely discuss the formidable obstacles and resistance to the centralisation of established bureaucracies.

[6] UNRISD: Dialogue about participation (Geneva) 1981, No. 1 p. 5.

[7] Md. A. Rahman: "Reflections", in Development: Seeds of change (Rome, SID, 1981, No. 1, p. 43).

[8] Economic Commission for Latin America: "Popular participation in development" in Community Development Journal (Oxford), Vol. 8, No. 3, 1973.

[9] Uma Lele: The design of rural development (Baltimore, Johns Hopkins University Press, 1975).

[10] F.A.N. Lisk: "Popular participation in basic-needs orientated development planning", in Labour and Society (Geneva), Vol. 6, No. 1, 1981.

[11] N.T. Uphoff and J. Cohen: Feasibility and application of rural development participation: A state of the art paper (Cornell University, 1979).

[12] WHO: Activities of the World Health Organization in promoting community involvement for health development (Geneva, 1982).

[13] Md. A. Rahman: "Concept of an inquiry", op. cit.

[14] Pearse and Stiefel, op. cit., p. 8.

[15] Uphoff and Cohen, op. cit. This text has become something of a standard work in terms of this particular interpretation of participation.

[16] This was a conclusion of the recent International Seminar on Popular Participation held in Ljubljana, Yugoslavia. See United Nations: Report of the International Seminar on Popular Participation (New York, United Nations Department of Technical Co-operation for Development, 1982).

[17] D. Curtis et al.: Popular participation in decision-making and the basic needs approach to development: Methods, issues and experiences (Geneva, ILO, 1978; mimeographed World Employment Programme research working paper; restricted), p. 1.

[18] WHO: Report on a WHO/UNICEF Intersectoral Workshop on Primary Health Care (Geneva, 1982), annex.

[19] idem: Activities of the World Health Organization in promoting community involvement for health development, op. cit., p. 6.

[20] C. Van Wijk-Sijbesma: Participation and education in community water supply and sanitation programmes (The Hague, IRC, 1981).

[21] See, for example, A.J. Ledesma et al.: 350 million rural poor: Where do we start? (Bangkok, United Nations Economic and Social Commission for Asia and the Pacific, 1980).

[22] FAO: Rural Organisations Action Programme (ROAP), Research guidelines and Participation of the poor in rural organisations (Rome, 1979).

[23] It could be argued that The peasant's charter (Rome, FAO, 1981) and the references therein to peasants' organisations fall within this category.

[24] We offer no specific reference here, as few references exist in the formal literature. In Chapter 3, case studies 3.3 and 3.4 are examples of this approach to people's organisations and the references presented there will be relevant.

[25] FAO: Participation of the poor in rural organisations, op. cit., p. 63.

[26] Md. A. Rahman: Participatory organisations of the rural poor (Geneva, ILO, 1977: mimeographed World Employment Programme, research working paper; restricted); D.F. Hodsdon: "The administration and activities of a young organisation of rural workers in India", in Agricultural Administration, Vol. 8, No. 4, July 1981.

[27] See, for example, case study 3.3.   The Bhoomi Sena example is perhaps the only detailed account available of this particular approach.

[28] United Nations Economic Commission for Latin America, op. cit.

[29] UNRISD: Dialogue about participation (Geneva) 1981, No. 1, p. 3.

[30] D. Curtis et al., op. cit., p. 6.

[31] W. Fernandes and R. Tandon (eds.): Participatory research and evaluation (New Delhi, Indian Social Institute, 1981), p. 5.

[32] P. Oakley and D. Winder: "The concept and practice of rural social development: Common trends in Latin America and India", in Manchester papers on development (University of Manchester, Department of Administrative Studies, 1981).

[33] A. Bhaduri and Md. A. Rahman (eds.): Studies in rural participation (New Delhi, Oxford and IBH Publishing Co., 1982).

[34] Pearse and Stiefel, op. cit., p. 4.

[35] FAO/ROAP: Participation of the poor in rural organisations, op. cit.

[36] K. Bhasin: Participatory training for development (Rome, FAO), p. 28.

[37] Several studies present lists of the kinds of obstacles/ factors which influence participation.   We reproduce two such lists here:

(a) Government policy
    Availability of external resources
    Decentralisation
    Availability of local leaders
    Traditional practices
    Willingness to change
    Awareness of benefits of
      participation
    Availability of communications

WHO: Community involvement in PHC (Geneva, 1977).

(b) Centralisation
    Lack of information/data
    Complexities of planning
      processes
    Costs
    Attitudes of planners
    Popular resistance to
      participate

United Nations: Popular participation as a strategy for promoting community level action and national development, op. cit.

[38] J. Cohen et al.: Rural development participation: concepts and measures for project design, implementation and evaluation (Cornell University, Centre for International Studies, 1977).

[39] G. Hunter: _A hard look at directing benefits to the rural poor and at participation_ (London, ODI, 1981).

[40] Pearse and Stiefel, op. cit.

[41] See note 37 above.

Chapter 3

THE PRACTICE OF PARTICIPATION

Our concern in this chapter is to examine critically a number
of examples of the practice of participation in order to further
our understanding of how it is implemented at the rural development
programme or project level.   Despite, however, the vast amount of
literature, the task is not as straightforward as it might appear.
This is because little of this literature actually deals directly
with the perspective of participation which is the subject of this
paper.   The literature on the "bigger" projects might describe in
detail the means of participation i.e. credit programme/farmers'
organisation, but few isolate the concept in any detail or analyse
its implementation.   On the other hand the literature on the
smaller, grass-roots project is non-conventional in nature and not
readily available.   In short we have very few well-written case
studies of participation in practice.   It is one thing to describe
the apparatus of participation;   it is another thing to state
beforehand a meaningful definition of participation and present an
analysis in those terms.   In fact this vast amount of literature
can be divided into four broad categories:

(a) studies of peasant/urban labour etc. movements which illustrate
     processes of social change and the increasing involvement of
     previously excluded groups from the wider society;

(b) works of a theoretical/conceptual level but which do not deal
     with implementation;

(c) studies on rural organisations where the emphasis is upon the
     establishing and the structuring of the organisation.   Parti-
     cipation within this context is limited to very few people and
     is not very helpful for considering more massive forms of
     participation;

(d) the greater part of the relevant project documentation presents
     participation as part of the project's objectives (i.e. water
     supply/package programmes).   However, this documentation does
     not tend to discuss participation in isolation, but often
     incorporates it into general project discussion.

The difficulty also is not the lack of examples of supposedly
participatory activities;   it is the lack of examples which are not

just a description of these activities but which establish beforehand an operational understanding of participation and, on that
basis, analyse and explain the activities.   In other words, reading
some of the case study material, it is very difficult to understand
clearly the study's working definition of participation which would
serve as an indicator of the project's success or otherwise.   All
this is, of course, a reflection of the general problem.   In too
many case examples it is <u>assumed</u> that the project activity will
bring about participation by its very action (for that is one of
its expected consequences) with the result that project implementation is explained in tangible (quantifiable) terms and not with the
intangible quality of participation, which seems to defy quantifica-
tion.   On the other hand, where the project consciously seeks to
explain its activities, in terms of some <u>process</u> of participation,
the material is not very substantial and thus our knowledge of how
to do this is still developing.

The selection of case studies is no easy task.   Our study did
not commission any field work which could be included in the text.
We are constrained by the material which is available.   There are
a number of case studies which supposedly illustrate the process of
participation but few contain the kinds of information wanted for
our analysis.   Also we have tried to avoid a situation where we are
limited to <u>one</u> particular text or article and have, in effect, to
base our analysis on that one source.   We have selected, therefore,
from the few case studies upon which there is a bit more material
in order to make our analysis more plausible.

In selecting our case studies we have tried to include examples
to reflect the differing interpretations of participation as discussed in Chapter 2.   In view of the FAO/ROAP study and the substantial documentation therein, we decided <u>not</u> to include a case
study on organisation as a vehicle of participation.   Where possible
we try with each of the cases to:

  (i) <u>examine the understanding of participation</u>;
 (ii) <u>critically review the methodology employed</u>;
(iii) <u>analyse the case's achievements in terms of participation</u>.

We shall conclude by analysing the substantive issues which arise
from our examination of the cases.   It should be noted that
section 3.2 is not a study of one particular rural health programme,
but a composite study of material on a number of cases.   Also the

Ethiopian experience is not a case study in the strict sense of the
term. We have interpreted the Ethiopian experience as a national
programme to bring about participation in rural development and
include in it the belief that it presents an interesting national
perspective of the concept under study.

3.1 Small farmer development programme (SFDP) - Nepal

Along with FAO/ROAP study and the recently established PPP,
the SFDP in Asia represents FAO's major commitment to the implementation of participation at the programme level. It was begun in
Nepal in 1975 and has since spread to other south-east Asian
countries. The FAO's involvement in the SFDP is based on the
assumption that people's participation in rural development depends
on strong support and commitment by government. The SFDP, therefore, is a combination of institutionalised credit, effective
delivery and group/organisational development, and it is aimed at
those disadvantaged groups in the Nepalese rural sector which
previously had little access to institutional support. The
original pilot project sought to motivate small farmers and landless
rural workers to form organisations of their own around a common
income-raising activity based on group work plans and group action
supported by credit and supervised by extension staff. The pilot
scheme was judged a success and by May 1979, some 370 groups com-
prising 3,992 small farmers had been set up.[1]

(a) Understanding of participation

The understanding of participation in the SFDP is based upon
three main elements: Organisation, delivery/receiving mechanism and
micro-level planning. Previously few of the small farmers and
landless workers of Nepal were in any either formal or informal
organisation. Without such organisation it is impossible for
development projects to make contact with such groups, because of
the administrative requirements of formal intervention and the need
for some kind of point of contact. The first task of the SFDP
programme, therefore, was to help to organise the small farmers into
structured groups. With the formation of organisation, the means
would exist for the functioning of the delivery/receiving mechanism.
The argument was that small farmers don't participate because they
don't have the structure to function as a receiving mechanism and,
therefore, are inadequate outlets for the delivery mechanism (i.e.
credit/extension services). If this mechanism could be instituted,

small farmers would be able to participate.   Finally the existence
of organisation and delivery/receiving mechanism means that the
small farmers can, within the context of the credit programme,
participate in discussing and planning the application of the credit
received.

Essentially the SFDP interprets participation in terms of
creating some assets for those small farmers previously economically
disadvantaged.   These assets and the strength achieved as a result
of development should enable these small farmers to seek and obtain
benefits from development programmes.   It is, therefore, participation in the benefits of development and evaluations would suggest
that, for the small farmers concerned, these benefits did accrue.[2]
This is in fact the way the studies on the SFDP explain the situation and less attention has been given to widening the perspective
in terms of a broader understanding of participation.   The participation is largely economic, or at least it is explained that way,
although references can also be found to other less tangible objectives which suggest that the group development might lead to the
small farmers attempting to transform their environment by collective
effort.   One important aspect of this is the _linking_ of the
different small farmer groups' efforts so that, with the greater
strength such linking could bring, more widespread pressure could
be put on the existing structure to deliver the development goods.

(b) Method

The two main elements in the SFDP method are the organisation
of groups and the work of the group organiser/action research fellow.
On the assumption that institutionalised credit is to be made available and the delivery mechanism can deliver the appropriate inputs,
the process begins.   It will be useful to look briefly but separately at these two elements:

Organisation of groups

The incentive for group formation is the offer of external
credit.   The groups become the receiving mechanism which seeks a
fair share of production inputs and services from the delivery
mechanism.   Although the delivery mechanism was directed towards
groups of men, women's groups were also set up within the SFDP.
The basic purposes of these women's groups were family planning,
training in weaving and nutritional education.[3]   They also provide
a structure for decision-making and management as well as helping

to safeguard members' interests through collective representation.
It is suggested that an optimum size for a grass-roots group is
between 15-20 members and it is emphasised that, in terms of composition, groups should be internally homogeneous.   The experience
to date has suggested a number of alternative bases for group
composition.[4]

The Small Farmers' Development Manual, which has resulted from
the experiences of the SFDP, details the processes involved in group
formation.   The key thing to note is that the groups are deliberately organised by an external body and do not emerge through
purely endogenous means.   This process comprises a number of basic
steps: checking availability of credit, village survey, selection,
formation, distribution of responsibilities and determination of
functions.   The group is by then established and functioning,
within the framework of established procedures and operations, as
the receiving mechanism.[5]   The groups are in fact the means by
which the small farmers participate in the development process.

Group organiser/action
research fellow (GO/ARF)

The GOs are the "initiators not the permanent crutches" of the
group development process.   In general terms the GO is seen as a
facilitator of the participation process.   He/she is not considered
permanent and, once the groups become "self-propelling", the GO is
expected to withdraw.   The GO's task is to "guide" the groups to
self-reliance, a state defined largely in economic terms.   The GOs
are assigned to work in a specific rural area and their main task is
the formation of the groups following the process outlined above.
The GO's duties are distinct from those of regular extension workers:
the GOs complement such workers but do not replace them.

The GO's basic relationship, therefore, is with the groups.
His/her involvement is close and the GO has a critical role in the
whole process of credit availability, group discussion and decision.
Clearly the issue of dependence cannot be overlooked here and the
SFDP Manual, conscious of this probable consequence, guides the GO
with "simple methods" to facilitate understanding and participation
by the small farmer.   Despite the crucial role of the GO, it is not
possible to find in the literature any indication or discussion of
the preparation needed to become a GO or of the skills or areas of
knowledge considered critical for the processes involved.   But
perhaps essentially the process is limited; if the credit is made

available, the GO facilitates the groups' access to it. The groups
appear to be formed very quickly, the GO goes into operation and the
delivery and receiving mechanisms come into contact.

(c) Analysis

Although a substantial manual has been written based on the
SFDP and a number of studies undertaken of the SFDP's operations,
there does not appear to be any kind of in-depth analysis of the
effects of the SFDP in terms of facilitating participation. The
reporting to date, and the evaluation commissioned in 1979, concentrate understandably on the quantifiable aspects of the programme,
i.e. numbers of groups/families, credit disbursed and production
increases. Some comment is made on the issue of participation but,
although just as important, it is less substantial than the quantifiable aspects. A review of this comment highlights the following
points:

(i) undoubtedly the group organisations have been a powerful
instrument in facilitating the access to development of
previously excluded groups. As more than one commentator
pointed out, however, continued access is dependent upon the
availability of institutionalised credit. It is uncertain
if the dynamism of participation could be maintained if the
credit faltered;

(ii) the issue of dependence on the GO/ARF is frequently referred
to. The groups are expected to become "self-propelling" and
seek further participation. But this will be impossible if
self-reliance is not developed;

(iii) much of the emphasis on participation is explained in terms
of small farmers' active participation in the groups, and
not necessarily their achieving of any effective participation
in the wider context of the Nepalese rural society;

(iv) the issue of self-propulsion is critical to assessing the
effective participation achieved by the SFDP. Otherwise
this participation becomes limited by existing institutional
arrangements.

The SFDP's impact upon Nepalese rural women has been limited to
activities of a traditional nature, as we referred to above. Recent
research has indicated the enormous burdens under which Nepalese
rural women toil and the vital contribution that they make to the

nation's agricultural development. This research concluded that the main problem is that not enough is known about how to address projects towards the specific needs of Nepalese women. The SFDP has certainly had some impact, but the obstacles to any kind of meaningful involvement by rural women in Nepal remain formidable.[6]

Although this evidence to date has tended to emphasise the tangible effects of the SFDP, some comment has been made upon the increasing participation. One study argues that the small farmers are no longer afraid to get involved:

> On the basis of their group strength the peasants are gradually coming out of their so-called culture of silence. They have a voice now to demand various services ... they are becoming members of local co-operatives in ever-increasing numbers ... and small farmers have been elected to local Panchayat bodies. Slowly but surely all this is increasing the strength of the poorest peasants vis-à-vis the big landholders and money-lenders.[7]

Undoubtedly the SFDP has given the poor some assets and also some economic strength. The key issue is to make this economic strength independent and self-sustaining. Effective participation for the Nepalese rural poor (both men and women) will come when they can have some meaningful influence upon development issues and decisions as a result of their own ability to participate.

3.2 Participation in rural health

In the past decade or so great efforts have been made to incorporate some notion of participation into rural health programmes. Much of the current literature on such programmes stresses the importance of participation to successful programmes and argues the inalienable right of rural people to have some say in the solution of their health problems. This literature does, however, understandably concentrate upon the health aspects of such programmes and the "participation" has not been readily understandable. Although our review of the material was limited, we would tend to have sympathy with the following statement:

> Community participation as an element of primary health care was not sufficiently brought out, because the ways in which the people take a direct part in discussions and in projects of interest to them are not clearly explained in most of the country reports.[8]

Even a complete text on a community health project in Ecuador, despite its title, proved elusive in actually understanding the mechanics of participation.[9]

(a) Understanding of participation

Although rural health programmes are a priority of many governments, the limited access by the rural people to established health
services is a common problem. Few governments, however, have the
resources to establish widespread rural health services. There
are also other reasons which explain this situation, and some of
these are cultural and based on the existence of traditional health
structures and practices. The more active participation of the
rural people is seen as a remedy to this situation. Such participation would be beneficial for a number of reasons:

  (i) make community financial and human resources available to
       government for rural health programmes;

 (ii) improve communications on health matters between government
       and people;

(iii) incorporate traditional health values, beliefs and structures
       into modern practice.

The emphasis currently is very firmly on encouraging and
actively promoting the participation of the people in rural health
programmes. The following WHO statement illustrates this concern:

> Community involvement for health development is understood
> to refer to a process to establish participation between
> government and local communities in planning, implementation
> and use of services in order to increase local self-reliance
> and social control over health care. Community involvement
> means that people, who have both the right and the duty to
> participate in solving their own health problems, have greater
> responsibilities in assessing the health needs, mobilising
> local resources and suggesting new solutions, as well as
> creating and maintaining local organisations.[10]

An interesting feature of the above statement is the use of the
term "involvement". It may be purely a semantic difference, but
perhaps the use of the term "involvement" signifies a particular
degree of participation. What does emerge from the various statements on community participation is that this participation is seen
as a vital ingredient in the provision of rural health services.
The involvement of the rural people is actively sought both in
terms of determining health objectives and in deciding upon an
appropriate course of action. This community involvement is indispensable to the success of a rural health project.

(b) Method

As rural health programmes are understandably more concerned
specifically with medical issues, the literature is less informative

on how participation is encouraged in such programmes.   There is,
however, no shortage of statements on the kinds of issues important
in encouraging participation, even if many of these statements are
very generalised.   The emphasis is more on what to do, rather than
how to do it.   For example, a study summarising the WHO work in
promoting community involvement in health development suggested the
following measures:

  (i)   delegation of responsibility to the local level of decisions
        on health care;

 (ii)   creation of community health councils;

(iii)   foster individual responsibility;

 (iv)   develop mechanisms for people to participate in national
        level health decisions.[11]

More specifically, a report from Ethiopia suggested the following
three key elements:

  (i)   sensitisation, awareness building and motivation of the
        community;

 (ii)   literacy and information campaigns;

(iii)   promotion of local health organisations.

If, however, one reads between the lines, a picture can emerge of
how community participation is encouraged.   A review of a number
of studies suggests that the following are key elements in stimulating this participation:

  (i)   intervention/survey: contact at the local level, seeking
        assistance from local officials;

 (ii)   explanation: of the health programme's objectives and
        congruence of those objectives with local needs;

(iii)   mobilisation/discussion: the stimulating of interest and
        awareness of the programme;

 (iv)   propaganda/campaign: spreading the knowledge of the programme;

  (v)   involvement: enlisting the support and help of local people:
        structuring local organisations as vehicles of this support;

 (vi)   delegation: continued involvement in maintenance health
        facilities and future health programmes.

     The above is not a model; nor are we suggesting that it is a
process easily discernible in all rural health programmes.   It

merely indicates the broad nature of the process and the stages involved. It is also an <u>official</u> process and reflects the activities of government-sponsored health programmes. We have not reviewed any literature on NGO-supported health programmes and so cannot comment on the relevance of the above to those programmes.

(c) <u>Analysis</u>

At a UNICEF/WHO workshop held in Mozambique in 1980, delegates reported on the state of community participation in health in their own countries. Interestingly in the socialist countries of Ethiopia and Mozambique it was reported that participation was being facilitated through local associations and the party structure. Elsewhere, and apart from Ujamaa in Tanzania, the reports were less encouraging. One country actually reported that participation was only a means of mobilising finance.[12]

In all cases, however, the association of participation with <u>mobilisation</u> was prominent, and this appears to be a key dimension in terms of rural health programmes. In other respects references to participation in rural health seem to lack supporting evidence. Statements, for example, which urge community involvement in national level health planning, whilst laudable, overlook the formidable obstacles of implementation which the literature rarely discusses. In rural health programmes there <u>is</u> consultation, there is discussion and there is considerable effort spent on seeking the involvement of the people. More active participation is related to the community directly assuming on-going responsibility for maintaining health facilities. However, it rarely involves the people participating in determining those <u>causes</u> of, and solutions to, their state of poor health which might lie outside the immediate concern of medical attention.

3.3 <u>Bhoomi Sena, India</u>

The Bhoomi Sena experience is one of the few of an entirely new genre of grass-roots examples which has been the subject of extensive study and thus provides information for analysis. For this reason we include it here. It is an example of an approach to working with previously excluded groups which is quite widespread elsewhere, principally in Latin America and the Asian subcontinent. We include it here, therefore, as illustrative of a more widespread movement.

The Bhoomi Sena (Land Army) Movement in the Palghar District
of Maharashtra State, India, is a spontaneous indigenous movement
forging a bond between the adivasis (tribals) and other poor groups
in the region into a united force.   The movement concerned itself
principally with the tribal men but, as it intensified, it touched
the women who, within tribal society, occupied an openly subordinate
position.   Over the years the adivasis gradually lost their land
to the moneylending sawkars.   In 1970 by a collective decision of
the adivasis this loss was resisted and crops seized.   Bhoomi Sena
was launched.   After the initial action, however, the movement
faltered and became enveloped in a programme of technical assistance
and financial paternalism.   This brief flirtation failed to tackle
fundamental problems and the Bhoomi Sena Movement re-emerged in a
new phase: the adivasis were now committed to taking action themselves to tackle these problems.   In 1976 Bhoomi Sena took this
new course and began a process which in the next three years spread
throughout the district.[13]

(a) Understanding of participation

In the context of Bhoomi Sena participation has been defined
as:

> "A process of creative social involvement by those concerned
> in defining and fulfilling their needs.   It is not a passive
> taking part in activities designed by others: nor an act of
> mere consuming the fruits of economic and social activity.
> It is the taking of initiatives to decide what is to be done
> and how, and to do it.

Participation is essentially concerned with power.   Bhoomi Sena is
concerned with mobilisation for political struggle as the only means
to give previously excluded groups any influence in the development
process.   Bhoomi Sena became "People's power" which implied
spontaneous collective action by the people, as opposed to centrally
directed action.   Furthermore, the assertion of the people implies
self-reliance, a process of breaking away from previous economic
and cultural ties of dependence.   To achieve this self-reliance,
organisation becomes important.   But not the type of organisation
which creates formal power, but one which reflects the will and the
interests of the people involved.

Participation in the Bhoomi Sena sense, therefore, is closely
identified with spontaneity and self-reliance, as opposed to formal
organisation and dependence which characterised previous efforts
to involve the adivasis in development.   This participation

expresses itself in the form of the people's struggle against oppression and exploitation, the assertion of their right to self-determination and the establishing of organisational forms which can release the people's creativity. It is in fact an exercise in liberation from the psychological and economic forces that have historically oppressed the adivasis and the emergency of a counter-vailing power to meet head-on the challenge of the forces. Partici-pation is not imposition or co-option but the empowering of previously weak groups with the collective strength to intervene to tackle their problems.

(b) Method

The Bhoomi Sena method is essentially one of "conscientisation". Readers may be familiar with this concept and aware of its import-ance in the writings of Paulo Freire and others. This is linked with Bhoomi Sena to the process of "endogenous knowledge-building" whereby the adivasis develop their knowledge in order to enhance their capacity for self-management of the tasks that confront them. Much has been written on the method of Bhoomi Sena which has been described as follows:

> ... To stimulate processes of collective reflection in which individuals are encouraged to articulate their own experiences, perceptions and thoughts, followed by collective discussion of what has been expressed, with a particular effort to understand the structural features of the experiences narrated that generate a commonality of individual perceptions.

The method reflects Freire's reflection-action (praxis) and is con-ducted within a framework of dialogue and collective reflection. An important instrument in this process is the shibir or camp for collective reflection. The object of the shibir is to share experiences and perceptions of oppression and to decide upon collec-tive action.   The shibir method became fundamental to the movement and different forms have been experimented with i.e. listening/ narrating and understanding/explaining.   At the shibir the adivasis did most of the talking whilst the organisational cadres initiated the discussion and sometimes attempted to give it direction. Finally the growth and spread of the movement necessitated some kind of organisational form to give it structure. As a result, adivasis's organisations Tarun Mandals were established.   In order to sustain the general struggle, these village level organisations were needed to help organise local effort.   But the initiative to establish a Tarun Mandal was at the village level and evolution was an autonomous process without central direction.

The controversial aspect of the Bhoomi Sena method (and an issue of debate within Freirian methodology generally) centered on the outsider. The outsiders in this sense were the organisational cadres that supported the movement. One study expressed the view of the Bhoomi Sena leadership on this issue as follows:

> We need outside help for analysis and understanding of our situation and experience, but not for telling us what to do.

The outsider must not offer ready-made solutions, but must first try to understand what the local issues are and help the adivasis articulate them. The principle should be one of minimum intervention, offering support and advice when required. The Vanguard (central cadre of Bhoomi Sena) has a supportive role to play but must not stultify the emergence of self-reliance.

(c) Analysis

The evidence suggests that in tangible terms the Bhoomi Sena movement has had considerable effect in Palghar district. This quantifiable effect has been threefold:

(i) the movement spread and took in more than the original villages in the Junglepatti area. In the three years 1975-78, the movement spread over 120 villages with a corresponding growth in the number of Tarun Mandals;

(ii) the process of conscientisation has resulted in action to tackle common problems. These included:
- freedom from labour bondage,
- implementation of minimum wage law,
- collective contingency funds;

(iii) the movement has grown sufficiently in strength for its candidate to seek successfully a place in the State Assembly in 1978.

The movement, in fact, influenced similar efforts in other parts of the State of Maharashtra where one of the authors visited two similar movements in 1980.

More qualitatively a recent study suggests that in the past decade the Bhoomi Sena movement has had a profound effect upon the position of tribal women in Palghar district. This study concludes that the tribal women have been "radicalised" by the Bhoomi Sena: molestation has ceased, forced labour has virtually ended and the women have gained a sense of self-importance and self-possession.

Although the study recognises the clear "social inequalities" that
tribal women continue to suffer, it argues that the fundamental
problems which the tribal women confront (i.e. minimum basic wage)
cannot be understood without consideration of the common problems
which they face with men as tribals.   Clearly a careful analysis
of the effect of a movement like Bhoomi Sena upon the historically
subordinate position of tribal women in India could teach us a lot
about how to face up to such an entrenched problem which is widespread throughout the Third World.[14]

Bhoomi Sena defines participation as the action of people
expressing themselves against oppression and exploitation and
includes the search for some kind of organisational form to spear-
head this participation.   It demonstrates that meaningful participation to be promoted requires that the people concerned understand
the complex social and economic relations of which they are a part.
In the process of understanding there must be a "redistribution of
thinking" and a rejection of the traditional notion that the people
have nothing to contribute.   Finally it asserts that participation
is unquestionably linked with the taking of <u>action</u>, on the basis
that such action should <u>not</u> be determined by others but should be
based on the people's own knowledge of the situation "at whatever
stage this happens to be".   The Bhoomi Sena movement is concerned
overwhelmingly with groups which previously have had no access to
any kind of development assistance.   Its approach and its efforts
highlight the formidable implications of the achieving of meaningful
participation by such groups.

3.4   Fisherwomen and participation - Brazil

The case study under review here is one of the many hundreds
of small, and in some cases individual, initiatives to further the
participation in the development process of previously excluded
groups.   Such initiatives are rarely recorded but together they
represent the network of non-government involvement in the development process.   This particular example is located in the village
of Bomtempo in north-east Brazil, a region described as the largest
underdeveloped area in the western hemisphere and where, despite
the advances of the Brazilian economy, poverty is endemic.   It is
an area which has been widely studied and in which successive
massive developments have failed to make much impact on the widespread poverty.[15]

Although agriculture is the dominant economic activity in
this part of Brazil, it is estimated that some 100,000 families live
primarily on fishing. Most of those involved in fishing are poor
and caught in the perennial trap between low production and small-
scale investment. They are organised into government-controlled
colonies supposedly to defend their interests. Some women also fish
to support the families' incomes. They fish separately and are more
restricted to the swamp areas along the banks of the river. Few of
the women have any education and, although most are married, they
receive little support from their husbands and have assumed the major
responsibility for feeding and raising the children. One report on
the group depicted their lives as follows:

> They are condemned to a life in the swamps, the sticky mud.
> They leave early in the morning with a basket, a comb and a
> bit of water and food. They head out in several crafts and
> are reality the basis of the swamp society. It is a life
> of work, struggle, some hope and a few jokes.

In early 1975 an _animateur_, who worked with a diocesan team, made
contact with the fisherwomen and began to work with them.

(a) Understanding of participation

In the context of the fisherwomen's group, the understanding
of participation is not dissimilar to that explained in case study
3.3 above. The _animateur_'s analysis of the women's situation confirmed their total marginalisation from any kind of development
initiative and their equally total lack of any resources to change
the situation. The _animateur_ had been brought up in the school of
conscientisation and analysed the women's situation in terms of
their fundamental inability to influence the forces that controlled
their lives. The women were in effect _powerless_ and lacked any
means to have a positive impact upon the forces that constrained
them. From the beginning therefore, the _animateur_ saw the basic
objectives for her work with the fisherwomen:

(i)   that the women should begin to assume the responsibility to
      direct their lives and not merely accept the direction of
      others;

(ii) that the women should regain some dignity in their lives;

(iii) that the women should begin to bring some influence to
      bear upon the fishing colony.

Participation, in the context of the fisherwomen's group, is a
process which develops over time. It also results from activities

designed to prepare and strengthen previously excluded groups to
become more actively involved. In this case the natural outlet
for this participation was the fishing colony. Yet the women had
previously been totally excluded from the colony, had no documentation and thus lacked a voice in, and access to, the organisation
that was supposed to represent them. Such participation cannot be
ordered or ordained; it has to be prepared. It is a participation not by invitation into the fishing colony, but as an expression
of right. Without access to some formal organisation of assistance
the fisherwomen would never have any hope of improving their lives.
The animateur's task was to work with the women in order that they
might establish a base in this formal organisation and have the
strength to participate effectively.

(b) Method

The case of this fisherwomen's group is one of the few examples
available where a record, although somewhat sketchy, has been kept
of the animateur's work over a period of time.[16] The animateur
began working with the women in 1975 and is still involved with them,
although the nature of her work has changed considerably. In trying
to understand succinctly the animateur's approach to working with the
fisherwomen, Galjart's statement is relevant:

> This approach entails intervention to facilitate the effort
> of relatively small, local groups in achieving, in a partici-
> patory manner, their development goals, and thus enhancing
> their members' life-chances, in spite of and in opposition to
> societal mechanisms and processes which influence these chances
> adversely.

The first two decisions the animateur took were not to impose
herself upon the women and not to proceed with any particular reference to time. She spent the first nine months merely observing the
women and being observed by them. One afternoon one of the women
stopped and spoke to her after a day's fishing. This was repeated
on successive days. Then the animateur was invited to fish with the
women - "my baptism in the mud" - and that evening sat and chatted
with them. The process had begun and continues today. If we
examine the animateur's approach to and work with the women in the
past seven years, we can discern a number of distinct states:

  (i)   a lengthy process of contact and building up of mutual
        confidence;
 (ii)   meeting group comes together;
(iii)   identification of issues - discussions on particular topics.

It is impossible to go into the detail of each stage or to suggest
a time-frame for each one.   The animateur stressed the patience
needed in building up links with the women.   Also little effort was
made to hasten or to formalise the group's structure.   Initially
there was no structure and meetings were held with a great air of
informality.   As, however, the group has begun to get involved in
the fishing colony, so a more formalised internal structure has
developed to direct this involvement.   The animateur herself
characterised her approach as having two main phases: descobrimento
(discovery) when animateur and group establish links between each
other and despertar (wake up) when the group's members began to understand the basis of their miserable existence and determined to do
something about it.

In view of the intangible nature of the processes involved and
the question of time, it is not easy to understand how the animateur
worked with the group.   The approach of her pedagogy is essentially
private, but is based on two main instruments:

- the group meeting;
- the dialogue.

Although there is an increasing amount being written about how one
should conduct the two instruments above, we have very little information on their practice.   This is because both are intimate and
personal processes which are difficult to record.   Texts may exist
which tell us theoretically how to run groups and conduct dialogue,
but the practice at the grass-roots level goes unrecorded.   We shall
return to this issue in Chapter 4.

(c) Analysis

In purely numerical terms the work of the animateur has resulted
in the increasing size and numbers of fisherwomen's groups in the area.
Sixteen women attended the first "formal" meeting in 1976; by 1981
the original group had grown to 45 and two other groups had been set
up, being a total of over 100 fisherwomen involved in group activities.
The groups are purposefully small to avoid the inevitable fragmenta-
tion of bigger groups.   Some of the original group members have been
responsible for diffusing knowledge among the local fisherwomen of
the existence of the group and encouraging new members.   In 1980
the first regional meeting of the different groups was held with 71
participants.

But the numerical results hardly reflect the real changes which
have taken place.   To encourage such groups to consider the issue

of participation actively, and then to undertake some kind of action
to get involved, is a daunting task. When the first formal meeting
of the group was held in 1976, there was little basis for encouraging
participation. After four years of the animateur's pedagogic work
with the women, the group felt that they were perhaps now ready to
get involved. What were the changes that took place to bring about
this situation? The answer lies in the difficult area of qualitative change and the role of subjective assessment in determining this
change. The animateur herself explains how she characterised the
fisherwomen's group in 1976 and again four years later:

Group in 1976	Group in 1980
No motivation	Feeling of solidarity
Accept paternalistic approach	Willingness to make an effort
Passive	Thinking outside immediate context
Suspicious	
Exploited	Better organised.

As a result of the above qualitative behavioural changes, the
group grew in strength and began to take steps to seek solutions to
their problems:

  (i)   a widespread movement began to get the women registered at
        the colony and to gain legal documentation;

 (ii)   progressive involvement in the colony's affairs culminating
        in the election of two women's representatives to the Board
        at the end of 1981.

The women's groups are part of a wider movement which encom-
passes over 5,000 people involved in fishing in north-east Brazil.
The work of the above animateur and her colleagues has increased
these people's involvement in their colonies and their access to
the colonies' resources. The colonies then pressurise for change.
The movement's most notable achievement has been federal legislation
to control the pollution that poisons the rivers they fish.

3.5 The structure of national
     participation - Ethiopia

The literature on participation refers to a number of examples
where, as a result of a radical societal revolution, newly-created
governments attempt in one form or another to incorporate the masses
in the development of the nation State. China, Viet Nam, Cuba and
Ethiopia are such examples. In each of these countries a socialist

revolutionary government has embarked upon a widespread campaign to associate the rural masses with the march of the revolution. Our task here is not to analyse or necessarily pass judgement on any of these socialist revolutions, but to examine one briefly in the context of the purpose of this paper.

The socialist revolutionary movement which began in Ethiopia in 1974 has its roots above all in the historical relationships between the Ethiopian landed élite, the land and the peasantry. Peasant protests and unrest occurred in pre-revolutionary Ethiopia and were highlighted as the incursion of capitalist development which led to land evictions and the general reduction of the peasantry to a marginal existence. The State and the Church were the biggest landowners supported by the landlords and their inter-mediaries. The peasants in the south were largely reduced to tenancy; in the north, although the communal landholding system gave the peasant access to land, he was still bonded by tribute to the aristocracy and the Crown. Land, the source of livelihood for the Ethiopian peasant, was almost wholly in the hands of others.[18]

In late 1974 the Provisional Military Administrative Council (PMAC) declared Ethiopian socialism. This stressed equality, self-reliance, the dignity of labour and the supremacy of the common good. In economic terms it stressed the need to socialise the means of production so as to eliminate the causes of differentiation and to promote the country's productive forces. In March 1975, a land reform was proclaimed and all rural land was declared the common property of the Ethiopian people. Immediately the effort began to organise the peasants for the part they were expected to play. In December 1975, a proclamation established the peasants' associations which were to be the main vehicle of peasant involvement. Women's associations were also established by the PMAC to represent and promote the interests of the rural women in Ethiopia.

(a) Understanding of participation

From the proclamation of Ethiopian socialism, the concept of greater peasant participation emerged as a cornerstone of the revolutionary process. In the first year the PMAC, launched an offensive to make contact with the rural masses and to begin the process of involving them in the revolutionary transformation. The peasants' associations were quickly proclaimed and, within a short space of time, thousands of associations had been formed. The peasants'

participation was couched in such terms as "collectivisation" and
later "co-operativisation" as the PMAC sought to institutionalise
a communal form of agriculture.

The process of peasant participation was presented as evolutionary and was governed by three basic principles: voluntary participation, mutual benefits and the strict application of democratic
centralism. The key word, of course, is the "voluntary" nature of
the participation which would imply that the peasants had a choice
to support the process of collectivisation or not. Essentially the
approach was to begin by establishing some basic forms of participation (i.e. peasants' associations) which would lead to some kind
of higher form with widespread collectivisation of production.
The peasants' world was in fact turned upsidedown overnight.
Previously they had been totally excluded from any form of involvement in the development of the Ethiopian State (apart from those few
who had become involved in capitalist development programmes, i.e.
CADU) but now they were being asked to participate actively in the
socialist revolution. The main parameters of that revolution had
already been drawn: the peasants were to be mobilised to give them
support.

(b) Method

The implementation of the Ethiopian socialist revolution began
with great speed. Resources were mobilised and the word of the
revolution was spread rapidly throughout the country. The PMAC's
first priority was to make contact with the rural masses and to link
their forces with the revolution's objectives. In this process the
objectives of Ethiopian socialism were explained. Initially the
enthusiasm was high and undoubtedly there was a feeling in rural
Ethiopia of participating in radical transformation.

In the process of institutionalising Ethiopian socialism, the
PMAC employed several means:

(i) the Zemecha: the mobilisation of over 60,000 secondary
school and university students. These students spread out
throughout the country making contact with the rural communities. Their immediate task was to explain and teach the
principles of Ethiopian socialism and initiate the formation
of the peasants' associations;

(ii) peasants' associations (PA): the lowest administration of
the State, the PAs were expected to co-ordinate administrative functions, agitate and mobilise the people to participate

in political and economic activities and maintain the
security of the region.   The PAs in effect filled the
power vacuum caused by the dismantling of the society.
They also were expected to combat the individualistic
tendencies of the Ethiopian peasant and help create the
structure for a socialist economy.

The establishing of the PAs proceeded at a rapid pace.   By late
1975, approximately 18,000 PAs had been formed: by the end of 1977
the number had risen to 28,583 with a membership of some 7.3 million
households.   The women's associations which were established became
dependent·upon the PAs in terms of their ability to give women access
to land.   The PAs' membership was based upon "heads of households"
and thus women had little direct access to or involvement in them.
The approach had been one of massive mobilisation within the context
of the newly-created PAs.   There was little subtlety in the process
and the Zemecha worked in teams, lived among the peasants, held
classes, explained and generally whipped up a sense of collective
involvement.   Later the process became more professional.   As the
PMAC moved towards co-operatives and the collective agriculture, so
trained cadres of promoters worked with the peasants instituting
these specific activities.

(c) Analysis

There can be no doubting the immediate initial impact of
Ethiopian socialism.   A dormant, feudal society was woken up almost
overnight and the message and apparatus of the revolution were
quickly spread.   There was in fact a "big thrust", a massive exercise in mobilisation which resulted in the nominal involvement of the
peasants in the peasants' associations, as we have seen from their
impressive numerical spread throughout the country.   But there was
little effort initially at political consciousness: the peasants'
associations and Ethiopian socialism were brought by the Zemecha and
the peasants nominally participated because the Zemecha required them
to do so.   Some studies have referred to the "authoritarian" attitude of the Zemecha students and to the dwindling interest in the PAs
once the initial mass mobilisation had run out of steam.

In terms of the impact of Ethiopian socialism on the position
of rural women in Ethiopia, recent studies suggest that little fundamental change has occurred.   Whilst increased agricultural production resulting from land reform might have helped the daily problem

of food supply, rural women are still dependent on their husbands economically, and therefore their position in Ethiopian society is still subordinate to men.   Efforts directed at women have tended to fall within the conventional practice of literacy and health campaigns.   Some "consciousness raising" has been achieved but much remains to be done if rural women in Ethiopia are to have some equal and meaningful access to the benefits of rural development.[19]

But the development of the PAs and the activities of the Zemecha only represented the beginning of a process which is currently assuming a more coherent structure.   The emphasis since 1978 has been upon the co-operativisation and the collectivisation of the Ethiopian peasantry; the transition to collective agriculture on the basis of co-operative production.   Few studies exist to show how this transition is occuring.   Yet experiences elsewhere highlight the difficulties of this transition.   The participation of the Ethiopian peasant in Ethiopian socialism has proceeded at a pace which is ahead of the peasants' psychological readiness for such dramatic changes.   The participation must be seen as evolutionary and supported at appropriate stages by experiences which will help the peasant accommodate to the change.   It is one thing to institutionalise the structure of participation and mobilise involvement; it is a different task to break down the centuries-old barriers to involvement and expect the Ethiopian peasant to make the transition overnight.

3.6 Comment

The case studies reveal both the different interpretations of participation that are practiced in the field as well as the enormous complexities involved in operationalising the concept. Participation is not an easily manipulable "thing".   Each of our case studies has revealed that it is a concept of many dimensions which have to be clearly understood before "participation" can meaningfully be used in the context of a rural development project. In none of the case studies can it be argued that "participation" had been achieved, apart from perhaps "participation" in terms of benefiting from the development project, i.e. SFDP/health programmes. Of course any such statement is based upon a particular interpretation of "participation".   In the SFDP/health programmes, for example, if we defined participation in terms of benefits and involvement in formal organisations, then some "participation" has occurred.

If, however, we define "participation" in terms of capacity for self-sustained development, then perhaps our conclusions might be different. We could reverse the analysis, for example, with the fisherwomen's case study.

Our purpose in labouring the point is to emphasise the multi-dimensional nature of the act of participation in a rural development project. We do this largely because so much of the literature does deal with "participation" as though it were some finite quantity which can be operationalised within the life-span of a project. Our case studies have revealed that this is to take a much too limited view of the complexities of participation and of the processes involved.

We have with each of the case studies analysed the nature of participation in the context of each project. It would be useful now to review these analyses jointly and to make a few general comments upon the practice of participation at the project level:

(a) the importance of research-action. The context of participation must be clearly understood before action is contemplated. This process of research-action must be built into the intervention mechanism;

(b) some form of organisation is fundamental to a process of meaningful participation. Without organisation the would-be participants lack a structure to facilitate the process;

(c) the critical role of the outsider in the process of participation. Apart from the rural health projects, in each of the other cases there was an agent/animateur/organiser whose role was to work specifically within the context of the process of participation;

(d) an inability to manipulate participation in terms of time. In none of the cases could we conclude that a state of participation had been achieved. We have still much to learn in terms of "measuring" participation and understanding directly its more tangible form.

Having reviewed the practice of participation in the context of existing projects, it is appropriate now to consider future strategy. In terms of the rural poor meaningfully participating in rural development projects, the experiences to date have not been very substantial. Could we learn something from our efforts to date and construct a relevant approach? To this issue we now turn.

Notes:

[1] There is now quite a considerable body of literature on the SFDP both in Nepal and in other countries in south-east Asia. It would be tedious merely to present a list here. The bulk of the literature has been brought out under the auspices of either the ILO or the FAO. Of particular use is the manual on small farmer development which has been produced as a result of the SFDP. See FAO: Small farmers development manual (Bangkok, 1978), Vols. I and II.

[2] A.J. Ledesma: 350 million rural poor: Where do we start? op. cit.

[3] In 1979 it was reported that there were ten women's groups associated with the SFDP. By 1981 this number had risen to 19 with a membership of 221. J. Joshi: SFDP Nepal (Bangkok, FAO, 1981), pp. 43-45.

[4] FAO: Small farmers development manual, op. cit., p. 21.

[5] ibid., pp. 21-28 for a detailed review of group formation, procedures and functions.

[6] ILO: Action to assist rural women in Nepal (Geneva, ILO, 1982; mimeographed World Employment Programme research working paper; restricted).

[7] D. Ghai and A. Rahman: The small farmers' groups in Nepal (Geneva, ILO, 1981; mimeographed World Employment Programme research working paper; restricted).

[8] WHO: Report on a UNICEF/WHO Inter-Country Workshop on Primary Health Care (Geneva, 1981), p. 21. It should be noted that section 3.2 does not relate to one particular rural health case study, but it is a composite reconstruction from a number of case studies.

[9] Ministry of Public Health (Ecuador) and Overseas Development Administration (United Kingdom): Community participation in family health (Quito, 1980).

[10] WHO: Activities of the World Health Organization in promoting community involvement for health development, op. cit.

[11] ibid., p. 6. A recent WHO trend report identifies the following key elements in mobilising community involvement: (i) gauging political commitment; (ii) building initiatives; (iii) decentralisation of decision-making; (iv) creating incentives; (v) incentives in health services; (vi) incentives for local communities.

[12] idem: Report of a UNICEF/WHO Workshop on Primary Health Care, Mozambique, 30 Mar.- 3 Apl. 1980 (doc. WHO/PHC/80/1); idem: Community involvement in primary health care: A study of the process of community motivation and continued participation (Geneva, 1977).

[13] The material for case study 3.3 has been drawn from a range
of written material on the Bhoomi Sena movement. The two principal
references are: (a) G.V.S. de Silva et al.: "Bhoomi Sena: A
struggle for people's power", in Development dialogue (Uppsala) 1979
No. 2, pp. 3-77; and (b) Md. A. Rahman: Some dimensions of people's
participation in the Bhoomi Sena movement (Geneva, UNRISD, 1981).
One of the authors of this study has also visited the area of Bhoomi
Sena and seen the effects of its work in terms of the growth of
similar movements.

[14] S. Mhatre: Multiple transition for tribal women: A study
of tribal women in Palghar Taluka, Maharashtra, India (Geneva, ILO,
1981; mimeographed World Employment Programme research working paper;
restricted).

[15] The material for case study 3.4 is almost wholly drawn from
project files and other documentation which have never been published.
One of the authors of this study has been closely associated with
the animateur and the group of fisherwomen over a number of years.

[16] This record has been kept as part of a joint research effort
undertaken by the animateur and one of the authors of this study.

[17] B. Galjart: "Counterdevelopment: A position paper", in
Community Development Journal (Oxford), 1981, No. 2, pp. 88-98.

[18] Case study 3.5 is drawn from a number of sources which
include: J. Markakis and N. Ayele: Class and revolution in Ethiopia
(Spokesman Books, 1978), and M. Ottoway: "Land reform in Ethiopia
1974-77, in African Studies Review, Vol. 20, No. 3, pp. 58-90. One
of the authors of this study was in northern Ethiopia from 1973 to
1976 and witnessed locally the changes which took place. See
P. Oakley: Tigrai rural development study: Social organisation
(Hunting Technical Services, 1976), Annex 8.

[19] Z. Tadesse: "The impact of land reform on women: The case
of Ethiopia", L. Benería (ed.): in Women and development: The sexual
division of labour in rural societies (New York, Praeger, 1982);
see also the report of an ILO/JASPA Employment Advisory Mission to
Ethiopia (ILO/JASPA, Addis Ababa, Sep. 1982).

Chapter 4

AN EMERGING STRATEGY

4.1 The basis of a strategy

It is widely argued that participation will not have much
meaning if it cannot be ensured that the rural poor can effectively
participate in rural development.   And yet despite the universal
commitment to participation, little progress has been made to date
in developing appropriate designs and organisational bases geared
to facilitate the participation of the rural poor.   It is certainly
not necessary to list the reasons why such participation has not
occurred, as it is highly improbable that readers of this paper
will not have some idea of what these reasons might be.   More
important is to consider whether a strategy to facilitate the participation of the rural poor in development might still be realistic
and, if so, the bases of such a strategy.

Before we turn to the content of this strategy, it would be
useful to reflect upon the framework within which many government-
supported participation strategies are conceived.   We have seen
that, although participation is a theme which has long historical
roots in the processes of rural development, it is in the last few
years, and particularly as a result ot the work of the ILO, UNRISD
and the FAO that its importance has been highlighted.   For example,
the WCARRD in 1979 declared:

> Rural development strategies can realise their full potential
> only through the motivation, active involvement and organisa-
> tion at the grass-roots level of rural people ... in concep-
> tualising and designing policies and programmes ...

This statement was interpreted in a strategy for participation
which stressed four important aspects:

- organisation of the poor;
- government decentralisation;
- planning at the local level;
- participation as the basis of rural development projects.

The above statement and strategy have been widely endorsed and are
influential in the consideration of future rural development initiatives.   Already the FAO has launched its People's Participation
Programme and within the United Nations system generally the agencies
are examining their work in the light of the WCARRD Declaration.

The situation, however, is still at the strategy level and there is still much to be done to provide the substance for a relevent approach to participation.

The WCARRD report identifies the fundamental dimension of participation which is concerned with power. The report clearly states that participation is "essential for the realignment of political power in favour of disadvantaged groups". The high-lighting of this dimension of participation is critical, even if the WCARRD does not suggest how such power might be achieved. The report is presented within the context of existing political structures and the assumption we must make is that meaningful parti-cipation can be stimulated in environments which previously did not help it flourish.

In the final analysis, it is difficult to disassociate "participation" from its relationship with power. As we saw in Chapter 2, this notion of power has been variously expressed. For participation to be meaningful, it must involve some direct access to decision-making and some active involvement in the determining of problems and practices. In the context of rural development projects it implies that the rural poor have some direct say in the policies and actions supposedly designed to improve their live-lihood. It is clearly evident that the rural poor of this world do not have any direct say in the policies and actions supposedly designed to improve their livelihood. "Participation" must be seen as an exercise of giving the rural poor the means to have a direct involvement in development projects. In other words they must be given the strength to be able to seek this direct involve-ment. Participation is not controlled collaboration: it involves working with the rural poor in order that they may be able to exert some influence upon the development that is going on around them. The only way that they will achieve this will be if they achieve some kind of power or authority which will allow them to influence events. Participation is to do with people meaningfully being able to have some influence, and for this to be so they must have some voice and some weight. The participation of the rural poor simply means giving the rural poor a chance to have some realistic chance to influence the decisions that affect their livelihood.

The issue, therefore, is how to mount a strategy of participa-tion based upon the above interpretation. Interestingly much of

the "official" literature is beginning to interpret participation
in terms of the above, but the strategies proposed present enormous
challenges given the pre-conditions which are established; i.e.
"... to facilitate this participation, decentralisation of government decision-making by strengthening supporting delivery systems
at the lowest level is required". We are not referring to the
considerable material which has recently been generated in terms of
projects actually reaching the rural poor: we are referring to the
radical scenario of the rural poor playing a direct and influential
part in the formulation and implementation of these projects.
Although this is the general tenor of the statements made, the
reality is that the rural poor do not as yet have any direct part
to play in rural development projects.

In considering an appropriate strategy we have to make one
major assumption: that the pre-conditions to participation as
expressed in the WCARRD documents are not going to occur in the
foreseeable future and that existing socio-political frameworks are
not going to facilitate meaningful grass-roots participation. We
must, therefore, consider a strategy that does not depend, for
example, on bureaucratic decentralisation or legislation to encourage local organisations, but which attempts to achieve participation
in the context of existing administrative frameworks. This would
seem to be the only available way of considering how the rural poor
might participate; the evidence to date is that the pre-conditions
as suggested have not yet emerged. We must consider, therefore,
how to bring about effective participation without waiting for the
structural changes generally indicated as indispensable.

4.2 Approach

The literature is growing on the many efforts in the different
continents to empower the rural poor and thus to bring about their
meaningful participation in rural development. There are a number
of examples of such efforts but as the approaches employed are still
largely experimental, there is little common terminology and
certainly no emerging universal model.[1] Moreover, it is the NGOs
who are more directly involved in this experimentation. We have
already suggested that the majority of government or "officially"
sponsored "participation" projects are more concerned with collaboration and benefits (which are tangible for some) than with
creating effective power for the rural poor. In the past decade or

so, therefore, it has been principally the NGOs who have pioneered an approach which aims to empower the rural poor. It is probable, however, that the FAO's recently launched People's Participation Programme and the innovative work with the rural poor being undertaken by the IFAD will in the future contribute to our understanding of a relevant approach.

If we accept the argument that most of the rural development projects supposedly aimed at stimulating the participation of the rural poor do <u>not</u> in fact lead to meaningful and effective participation (i.e. <u>not</u> simply in the benefits of a development project) then perhaps we can understand two important features which characterise rural development projects which do seek effective participation:

(a) project activities to bring about this participation are an <u>end</u> in themselves and the project is designed and staffed to this purpose;

(b) these activities are seen as an essential and necessary foundation to activities of a more economic nature.

In other words we cannot <u>assume</u> that participation will occur merely as a result of project intervention. The "preparation" of the rural people to participate effectively must be seen as an important project activity in itself, both apart and preceding activities of a purely economic nature. The "participation" of the rural poor must become the fundamental objective of the project, as upon that effective participation can then be built the more tangible economic activities. The evidence would suggest that where projects have tried to stimulate "participation" as a result of economic activities, this "participation" is limited to the few, is more concerned with benefits and does not enhance the rural poor's chances of effectively participating in the development going on around them. The process of empowering, of giving strength and a basis for future involvement must be considered as a priority project activity.

A review of a number of such projects in different continents in the first instance reveals a number of common key concepts which characterise the approach employed. We present them here in no systematic order, but more to show the important elements in an approach to effective participation:

(a) the <u>process</u> nature of such project work, in which it is difficult to establish fixed, quantifiable parameters;

(b)   the disaggregation of the rural poor and the identification of discrete socio-economic <u>groups</u> as the basic unit of development; (the term "group" is used here to encompass a range of practice from informal, unstructured gatherings of rural people around a common purpose to the more structured formal organisations of the rural poor);

(c)   the notion of <u>bottom-up</u> with the absence of any pre-determined models and the emphasis upon the emergence spontaneously of a relevant approach from below;

(d)   the principle of <u>self-reliance</u> and the need to reduce a development based upon dependence;

(e)   the issue of the <u>control by the groups</u> concerned of the development project activities;

(f)   the importance of collective action by the group to tackle the problems which they confront.

This list is <u>not</u> presented as any kind of charter or guiding faith and would not necessarily be acceptable to the different projects we examined. We present them here in order to characterise the nature of the approach, before later examining its method in more detail.

In some cases the basic elements in the approach adopted have been spelt out in a bit more detail and give us a clearer insight into the project's activities. It is not possible to distil from these examples any kind of common framework of approach, even though there are similarities. It would appear that different projects are experimenting with the same broad approach in different parts of the world, which provide us with a richness of material even if none has yet reached (or may ever reach) the stage of becoming a replicable model. We have decided, therefore, merely to reproduce a few cases here to illustrate the nature of the work in progress. We shall not discuss them individually in detail but simply show the main elements in the projects' approaches to achieving participation through empowering:[2]

(i)   self-interest
     from simple to complex
       militancy
     the tactics of the powerless
     project agent and problem
       identification
   (PHILIPPINES)

(ii)   mobilisation
      conscientisation
      assertion
      organisation
      (INDIA)

(iii)	training	(iv)	critical faculty
	mobilisation/conscientisation		participation
	consolidation/expansion		organisation
	organisation		solidarity
	interaction		articulation
	(SRI LANKA)		(BRAZIL)
(v)	community action	(vi)	preparation/research
	involvement of poorer sections		training
	no permanent dependence		reflection
	technical appropriateness of project work		action
	(INDIA)		(MEXICO)

Although the range of terms employed is wide, there is a remarkable similarity in the above frameworks. Some of the cases, (ii), (iii) and (vi), indicate not only the main elements in the approach but also the sequence of action. The others express more the broad principles with no reference to their relative positions in terms of project implementation. Each approach of course is a product of its particular context and as such it is not possible to contrast and compare. Each has been designed in terms of a specific set of circumstances and their relevance can only be judged within these circumstances. Although, however, the approaches are context specific, we can identify a number of common issues. All of the above approaches, whilst incorporating "economic" activities within the context of the project, are fundamentally designed towards achieving some kind of power or more effective involvement for the rural poor. Also in each of the above cases, the "target group" was small farmers, tenants or the landless who share the common problem of marginalisation and lack of access to resources. Similarly each of the approaches does not express any notion of time. The ultimate aim of the project is expressed in terms of "empowering" and the main elements are described, but little indication is given of the time which the process of empowering takes.

It is intriguing that such relatively similar approaches to the problem of the rural poor have emerged in different continents. Interestingly, and apart from some animation rurale work in West Africa, there is little evidence of the widespread occurrence of an "empowering" approach in that continent, unlike Latin America and the Asian subcontinent. These approaches, therefore, are illustrative of a fairly widespread practice to "empower" the rural poor. We should now turn to examine the methodological basis of this work.

4.3 Method

We are concerned in this section to try to understand <u>how</u> a process of effective participation is brought about.   In this respect it is true to say that the literature on Bhoomi Sena is the only detailed and widely available methodological account of this work.   There is a vast amount of non-conventional literature from different project sources, but it is scattered, and the time available has not permitted any systematic analysis.   One common feature of this literature is that it is highly descriptive: our knowledge of how to explain the process of empowering in the context of rural development projects is still unclear and hence projects tend to emphasise the detail of project activities rather than an analysis of those changes in terms of empowering.

We have, however, examined a number of projects and tried to explain their inherent method in terms of a process with a series of stages or phases.   This form of analysis is used to highlight the nature of the process and to show the different activities associated with each stage.   We <u>cannot</u> look at a process of participation in the same way that we look at, for example, the extension of a new credit programme; we must understand its essentially evolutionary nature and try to identify the main stages of this evolution.   The following are a number of examples of the methodological approach to participation in a number of projects:

(i) selection of target audiences
     formation of groups
     action inside the group
     action outside the group
     autonomy of group
     (BRAZIL)

     identification of group
     contact with training centre
     leadership training
     formation of groups
     group development
     (BANGLADESH)

     study
     creation of groups
     training
     group decisions
     collective action
     (SENEGAL)

     approach/contact village
     spread contact in village
     survey
     discussion
     decision to tackle problems
     building up of confidence
     decision of action
     action committees formed
     (INDIA)

     economic improvement
       activities
     promote receiving mechanism
     stimulate linkages with
       servicing agencies
     (PPP)

Each of the above examples demands, of course, detailed analysis, which could only be done effectively through field work. They are presented merely as sketches of the method implicit in participation projects. Although we can note some similarity of terms used (i.e. formation of groups/taking of action) each of the above methods is specific to a particular context. It would suggest, therefore, that there can be no universal model for stimulating participation at the project level but that also experiences are not so dissimilar that we cannot at least suggest some common elements. We could analyse the examples above and suggest that there are four principal stages to the methodology involved:

- contact with target group;
- process of group structuring and formation;
- preparation of work with group in terms of their future participation;
- action to implement the participation.

The above is a purely hypothetical framework, although a detailed analysis of project documentation would support the relevant, if not the relative, importance of each of the stages. We could now enter into more detail by examining a number of common features of the above framework.

4.3.1 Pedagogy

The process of empowering for participation is essentially a non-formal educational activity. Participation is indeed an educational process but one in which the conventional nature of education is turned upsidedown. A number of terms have been used to describe this educational process, the more common of which are "education for liberation" and "conscientisation". The form of education becomes a process by which a person who previously has been the mere object and passive recipient of knowledge is transformed into the subject and active creator of knowledge. It is a radical departure from the classical, formal educational approach, and it seeks to liberate individuals from the environment which constrains them.

It is only in the past decade that such a form of education has been experimented with at the rural project level. Although the practice is increasing, there are few substantial studies which give us an insight into how such an educational approach works.[3] Much of the experience to date is restricted to project files. However, an examination of some of these files reveals a number of important elements in this pedagogy:

(a)   it is <u>non-directive</u> and seeks not to impose knowledge and ideas
      but to explore the rural poor's socio-political environment in
      order to structure an understanding of the problems to be
      tackled;

(b)   it is essentially a <u>dialogical</u> process, in that it seeks
      discussion on equal terms and not, in the more conventional
      extension model, the direct communication of pre-determined
      ideas;

(c)   the key role of the <u>agent</u> whose task is to accompany the process
      and support it accordingly (see 4.3.3);

(d)   the importance of small economic/physical <u>projects</u> as a means
      of furthering group activities and encouraging participation.[4]

      There is a great richness in project files on the pedagogy of
participation but little as yet has been systematically analysed.
There is also a great amount of improvisation, with commitment to
a philosophy but little apparent coherent approach.   Where we can
understand a bit more is when we examine the <u>instruments</u> of the
pedagogy.   These straddle a broad and imaginative range and include:

(a)   the group <u>meeting</u> which is held on a regular basis and which
      is the basic forum of the pedagogy of participation;[5]

(b)   training sessions and study seminars which serve to develop
      the process of conscientisation;[6]

(c)   the use of social <u>drama</u> to highlight a particular issue and
      provoke involvement in analysis and comment;[7]

(d)   simulation or other such <u>games</u> based upon the analysis of a
      common issue.[8]

The pedagogy of participation is a highly individualistic experience
which, whilst we can identify common elements and principles, is
often so bound up with the individuals concerned that the sharing of
the experience becomes difficult.   A major task will be to devise
a means to <u>monitor</u> appropriately the pedagogy in practice so that we
can begin to put this experience to wider use.

4.3.2 <u>Groups</u>

      Apart from the more common identification of health programmes,
for example, with the rural community, there is an increasing awareness that the community or village, geographically expressed, is an

over-aggregate and needs to be broken down.   In the past few years
discrete socio-economic groups have become the targets of rural
development intervention.   In three of our case studies we noted
the emphasis upon groups.   Also the basis of FAO's new PPP
strategy is organised groups of the rural poor.   There is at this
moment a lot of experimentation with groups in rural development
projects, and this experience can be divided into two broad
approaches:

(a)   the use of the groups as a basis for economic "take-off"
      which will enhance the prospects of participation;   and

(b)   the use of the groups to build up an organisational form and
      collective solidarity as precursors to participating in
      economic development.

Neither approach is mutually exclusive and much of the practice
contains elements of both of these approaches.   Our review of
this practice would suggest, however, that in each case one of the
above approaches is dominant.   Both approaches have the common aim
of the greater "participation" of their members in rural development, but they differ in terms of the way in which they see the
groups achieving this greater participation.

      The argument for the use of groups in achieving the partici-
pation of the rural poor in development stems to some extent from
the inability of previous institutional forms (i.e. co-operatives)
to facilitate this participation.   It also reflects the "changing
paradigm" of development thinking and the realisation that development aimed at the "community" in general inevitably resulted in the
benefits accruing to the better-off and more powerful sections of
that community.   There now appears to be a general consensus that
if rural development is to reach those previously excluded sections
of the rural population, it must be purposefully directed towards
clearly identified and discrete groups within that excluded section.

      Although the use of groups in extension method, for example,
is no novelty in rural development, the present practice is radically
different.   Much of the more conventional use of groups reflects
the influence of group dynamics and the North American method of
rural extension.   The current experimentation is a radical departure
in that it uses groups as the dynamic focus of intervention and
deliberately aims to strengthen a particular group in order that it
might be in a position better to defend its interests vis-à-vis other

groups as well as more successfully compete in the access to
resources.   The intention is implicit in much of the current
practice and certainly characterised the groups in the case studies
we reviewed.

At this juncture it is not possible to offer any kind of formal
definition of the kind of "group" to which we are referring.   The
literature on group dynamics can offer us a range of scientifically
acceptable definitions, and these can help structure our knowledge.
The practice with groups in terms of the context of this paper is
still developing, and as yet no universally applicable format has
emerged.   However, if we review the practice to date, we can
identify a number of critical issues in terms of the use of groups
for rural development:

(a) Formation: the initiative in forming groups for participation
     in rural development is a critical issue which will determine
     the nature and course of the group's development.   The issue
     is whether in fact that initiative comes from outside and is,
     in effect, imposed on the individuals involved.   For meaningful
     participation the emphasis should be put on the emergence of
     the group structure as a result of pedagogic processes.

(b) Membership: the practice here is wide and varied, but does
     seem to be generally based on some concept of common economic
     interest as the basic criteria for group composition.   The
     "rural poor" is too broad a category in this respect, and the
     level and nature of economic activity is a more accurate basis
     for membership.   Both men and women are given equal member-
     ship.   Groups are also small in size and the common practice
     is to limit their numbers to between 15-35 members.

(c) Structure: the group must achieve some form of internal
     structure in order to give it the organisational base from
     which to seek participation.   Again the critical issue here
     is whether the structure is in fact imposed from outside or
     whether it develops as the group develops.   To avoid the
     dependency which inevitably results from structures which are
     suggested or imposed, emphasis should be put on allowing the
     members to fashion the organisation that most suits their needs.
     In this respect also the issue of leadership is equally diver-
     gent. Conventional group strategy is still psychologically
     tied to the concept of the benevolent leader among his or her
     peers; a more radical alternative encourages the emergence
     of leadership as the group develops.

There is now a growing and rich project literature on the use of groups to bring about some form of participation, but we still lack a major research effort to analyse the experience to date. The process involved is complex and cannot be subsumed within a rural development project's other activities. The development of strong and economically viable groups represents a major opportunity to achieve meaningful participation for the rural poor, but their development must be deliberately encouraged. An idea of the processes involved is highlighted in the following diagramatic representation of the stages of group development:

Stages	Characteristics
Initial contact	Confidence
	Friendship
Intermediate stage	Group structuring
	Membership
	Solidarity
	Internal participation
Principal stage	Formalisation
	Organisation
	Collective deliberation
	Action

The above is _not_ presented as a model but merely as an indication of the dimensions of group development. If we argue that the development and strengthening of groups is fundamental to the rural poor achieving some form of participation, we must be aware that, to be authentic and self-sustaining, the development of such groups must be a major task within any rural development project.

4.3.3 Agent of participation

In each of the case studies we noted that a critical role in the process of participation was assigned to the project agent. A variety of different names have been used for the agent. The WCARRD Declaration referred to _animateurs_; the SFDP and the PPP refer to _group organisers_, whilst in Latin America the more common term is _agent_. Whatever the name adopted, there is agreement that the process of group development and participation must include an agent to facilitate the process. Indeed it is argued that such an agent is vital to the success of the process. The use of grass-roots agents is, of course, not new in rural development; village

level and community development (CD) workers were (and still are) a
dominant feature of much of the rural development of the 1950s and
1960s.   In this respect it is pertinent to ask in what way agents
of participation are different from the more traditional CD worker.
The answer lies in the difference of the role of a CD worker as a
harmoniser of interests at the community level, and his/her work
with the community élites, whereas the agent is more concerned to
stimulate deliberately the awareness and the development of disadvantaged groups.

We are, therefore, concerned with examining the role of the
agent in the process of participation, which we define in terms of
a process of empowering.   The agent, almost inevitably, will not
be from the group, and thus we confront the issue of the outsider.
In this respect the literature on Bhoomi Sena is one of the few
written examples available of the agent in this process.   Other
studies have listed functions of the agent, but these invariably
refer to the more tangible activities and procedures of contact,
information on group or assistance with setting up small projects.
Indeed all this is usually expressed in such terms as "duties" or
"tasks" and stress the bureaucratic nature of the agent's activities.[9]
Such lists of "duties" would appear to reduce the agent to a general
CD worker and they fail to stress the critical pedagogic role of the
agent in assisting the group to acquire strength.   There is no doubt
that in a process of meaningful participation, the agent's role
cannot be explained in terms of a list of "duties".

It would appear, therefore, that there are two different
practices of the role of the agent in participation, and this difference has implications for skills and training:

(a)   projects where the agent's role is primarily to facilitate the
      access of the group to resources for development;   and

(b)   projects where the agent's role is primarily to develop an
      appropriate pedagogy to stimulate awareness within the group
      and thus begin a process of the group seeking active partici-
      pation in development.

Whilst the two roles do have some complementarity, they also involve
different personal characteristics and skills.   Ideally the two
roles should demand two agents but, given the pressure on resources,
the two roles are often incorporated into one.   Both the ILO and
the FAO are associated with projects in which these two roles are

combined.[10]   With (a) we are talking in terms of an agent whose
role is to facilitate the access of groups to government projects
and resources: with (b) we are talking of an agent whose principal
activity is to build up the strength and the organisational base of
groups of the rural poor.   In terms of the former role we note many
similarities with the role of the old CD worker: with the latter,
and particularly in the context of formal rural development projects,
we are talking about a very different person.

Again, we come up against the problem that much of the experimentation with agents of participation in the latter sense is to
be found only in project files and documentation.   Little formal
published material has explored this type of agent.[11] A detailed
analysis of such files would be instructive.   However, if we consider the agent's role in terms of the pedagogy of empowering, then
there are a number of areas which would merit further examination:

(a)   characteristics/selection: It could be argued that selection
      is critical in that unless an agent possesses certain necessary
      characteristics, he or she would be inappropriate to the work
      involved.   If characteristics such as humility, commitment,
      sensitivity and self-confidence are attributes considered vital
      to most rural development workers it is difficult to see how
      such characteristics can be transmitted through training;

(b)   skills: In terms of the processes involved, the agent needs
      the ability to communicate, both verbally and non-verbally,
      and also to analyse and diagnose the context of his work with
      the rural poor;

(c)   training: It is impossible to avoid the conclusion that there
      can be no formal training as such.   Case experience suggests
      that agents are best prepared for the work by learning by
      experience.   Seminars and meetings help to structure the
      continual experience, but there exists no formal course for
      the training of such agents.

It would not be difficult to construct a list of "tasks" for
agents of participation to undertake, a list of the supposed
qualities such agents should possess or a hypothetical training
course to equip them with the relevant skills.   Such an exercise,
however, would only contribute to the extensive documentation
already available on those issues and would leave us none the wiser.
There can be no doubt that the project agent is a critical element

in the process of participation and that the <u>critical dimension</u> is
his role with the group in building up its organisational base, its
internal solidarity and its potential actively to intervene in the
development process.   And yet we still know so little of the nature
of this role, the content of its function, the areas of knowledge
required for its performance and the ways in which it can be
developed in agents.   The manuals of the past are not useful in
this situation and merely to transfer established techniques of CD
work to the process of participation is to misunderstand the complexities of the process.

4.4 <u>Evaluation</u>

It is appropriate also in this chapter to consider the issue
of the <u>evaluation</u> of rural development projects in terms of whether
or not they result in the meaningful participation of the rural poor.
In this sense we are <u>not</u> necessarily talking only of "participatory
evaluation", although the approach implicit in that term will surely
be relevant.   We are more concerned with the means to be able to
form a <u>judgement</u> upon whether a particular rural development project
has resulted in participation, the nature of that participation and
the magnitude of the achievement in terms of the resources employed.
We are all rightly concerned to understand the "economic impact" of
rural development projects and to measure that impact accordingly.
It is equally important to be able to judge the impact of a project
in terms of participation.

At this moment, however, we have very little material available
to guide us on this crucial issue of the "evaluation" of participation.[12]   Practically no research has been done on the question of
judging the effect of rural development projects in terms of whether
they do, or do not, result in participation.   The difficulties are
compounded by the complexities of "participation" and the inadequa-
cies of conventional project evaluation techniques.   In the context
of the recently launched PPP programme of the FAO an initial study
has considered this issue of evaluation, and presented us with a
tentative framework for the monitoring and evaluation of the PPPs.[13]
If we consider the complex problem of the evaluation of participation,
two issues should be noted:

(a)   in evaluating "participation" we are concerned with forming a
      judgement on <u>processes</u> which are <u>qualitative</u> and not results
      which are quantitative;

(b) the approach to such evaluation, therefore, is more concerned with <u>description</u> and <u>interpretation</u> than with measurement and prediction.

The main difficulty in this evaluation is <u>how</u> to give some kind of <u>form</u> to the process of participation. Unless the "participation" can be expressed in intelligible terms it will defy all efforts at judgement. Superficial efforts have confronted the issue by attempting to quantify and put a tangible measure on participation (i.e. <u>how many</u> members, frequency of attendance at meetings, etc.) but these dimensions do <u>not</u> adequately reflect a very complex process. It is true to say that adequate techniques have not yet been developed by which we could "measure" the element of participation in a rural development project. We have a better understanding, however, of the complexities involved, which suggest the following as the critical areas we need to understand:

(a) valid <u>criteria</u> for understanding the nature of the element of participation in a rural development project;

(b) a set of <u>indicators</u> which would give <u>form</u> to the above criteria and thus help to express "participation" in intelligible terms;

(c) appropriate <u>methods</u> at the project level, for monitoring the above indicators and maintaining a continuous record of the unfolding process of participation;

(d) the <u>interpretation</u> of the information recorded in terms of making a judgement concerning participation.[14]

The measurement of the non-material objectives of rural development projects presents us with formidable conceptual and analytical problems which we need to tackle if we really do wish to form a judgement on "participation". It is <u>not</u> enough merely to apply conventional evaluation techniques and to present participation in quantifiable terms; but we have a formidable task ahead if we wish to develop appropriate techniques for measuring the non-tangible nature of participation.

4.5 Project activities

Inevitably at some time during the process of participation some kind of economic activity will be undertaken by the group. We have seen already a divergence of practice in this respect. Either such activities are used as the means to creating assets and greater economic strength in order to allow the group more effectively to participate in development, or such activities are used as the means to stimulate group involvement, solidarity and the development of the capacity of the group to take action. Whatever the ultimate purpose of the activities, they do play a central role in the process of participation.

It is not our intention to review the mechanics of such activities or to analyse their effects to date. We are more concerned here with understanding the basis upon which the activities are undertaken in such a way that they strengthen the process of participation. These economic activities should not be undertaken in a purely mechanical way but must be consciously related to the ultimate objective: the strengthening of the process of participation. If we review examples of the practice of such activities, therefore, we can suggest the following principles which should guide implementation.

(a) involvement: the group concerned must be involved in the basic aspects of project formulation, decision-making and implementation, and the whole operational base of the project must be organised with this principle in mind;

(b) minimise dependence: every effort must be made to minimise the dependence of the activity, either in material or human terms, on materials from outside, otherwise group autonomy will never be achieved;

(c) sustainability: the activity must be able to be sustained in the context of locally available resources. It must represent an initiative which can be taken up by the group itself and further developed. In other words, it must not be beyond the capabilities of the group;

(d) next step: similarly the activity must represent what technologically is the next step for the group, and not be a technological advance which is beyond the natural development of the group;

(e) effective as opposed to "efficient": it will be perhaps necessary in the short term to forego our slavish adherence to the economic principle of efficiency, and undertake economic activities which are an effective use of resources and can bring about some economic advance, although they may not represent the most efficient use of those resources.

Although the economic activities of participatory projects are not a central issue of this study, we were concerned to emphasise that the basis upon which such activities are undertaken is critical to the process of participation. We do not offer the above basis of operations as a model universally applicable. Experience would indicate, however, that if a central objective of the activity is, in one way or another, to develop the group's ability to participate, then thought and care must be given to the way in which the activity is undertaken. Project activities in the context of a process of participation cannot be undertaken in a purely mechanical way.

4.6 Comment

In this chapter we have tried to put a little substance into what appears to be an emerging strategy based on an extremely fragmented practice and experience. In the past five years or so various statements have been made on the overall nature of a strategy for participation.[15] We have also seen the concern with participation reach into the areas of research and evaluation. "Participatory research" and "participatory evaluation" reflect the emergence of this new strategy and they are key activities within the process of participation. There is now a growing literature on both of these issues in conceptual terms.[16] There is indeed sufficient evidence of a widespread practice of some kind of strategy of participation to be able to affirm that the search for such a strategy is seriously afoot. In relation to the quite considerable practice, however, our recorded knowledge is very limited and not readily accessible. It is time to mount an exercise to pull the varied practices together and to understand better the implicit strategy. In this chapter we have merely presented the framework of a strategy for effective participation. Much of our framework demands further inquiry and substantiation, but we believe that the practice to date is sufficient for us to argue that the framework is valid.

One conclusion, however, is that if we do associate the concept of participation with some idea of power (whichever way this power is expressed), we really do have to think of a radically different concept of project practice. The dominant paradigm of experts generating proposals and the rural poor passively acquiescing in one way or another, must be broken and replaced by entirely different actors. The priorities become the building up and the strengthening of people, an approach which demands radically different project agents, as opposed to the too familiar emphasis upon

tangible activities. To speak of seeking to achieve meaningful
participation without considering a fundamental shift in the nature
of practice is quite meaningless. But that is the implication of
a strategy of participation.

Notes:

[1] Whilst the literature on this experimentation is still
largely non-conventional and we have few substantial texts, a
number of them indicate the main parameters of this experimentation
and the terms employed. Md. A. Rahman: "Concept of an Inquiry",
in Development: Seeds of change (op. cit.); Xavier Institute:
Development from below (Ranchi, Institute of Social Service, 1980);
W. Fernandes (ed.): People's participation in development (Indian
Social Institute, 1981); K. Constantino-David: "Issues in community organisation" in Community Development Journal (Oxford), 1982,
No. 3.

[2] The material for four of these examples is drawn from unpublished project files and other documentation. The examples from
the Philippines and Sri Lanka are taken from Md. A. Rahman (ed.):
Grass-roots participation and self-reliance: Experiences in south-
east Asia and the Pacific (forthcoming).

[3] Probably the most complete study of the pedagogy of participation undertaken to date is the one published by the Centre for
International Education based upon a case study in Ecuador. The
three principal texts in this series are: A.W. Etting: Characteristics of facilitators: The Ecuador project and beyond; J. Hoxeng:
Let Jorge do it: An approach to rural non-formal education; and
W.A. Smith: The meaning of conscientizacão: The goal of Paulo
Freire's pedagogy. All are published by the Centre for International Education, University of Massachusetts.

[4] P. Oakley and D. Winder: "The concept and practice of rural
social development: Current trends in Latin America and India, in
Manchester papers on development (op. cit.).

[5] The meeting of the group is the critical forum for its
development. And yet the group does not necessarily develop on the
lines of conventional group dynamics practice. One outsider, who
experiences a series of group meetings in one project area, commented:

> In these meetings there is no co-ordination, no leadership,
> no agenda, no timetable. It is a meeting which begins without
> beginning, and ends without ending. A strange meeting. If
> there was somebody present trained in group dynamics, his mind
> would be confused. The meeting is seen, lived and felt as the
> supreme event of the community. What is decided in a group
> meeting can only be changed or corrected in a meeting.

(Quoted in Oakley and Winder, op. cit.).

[6] See, for example, K. Bhasin: Breaking barriers: A south
Asian experience of training for participatory development (Bangkok,
FAO, 1979).

[7] A comprehensive example of the growing literature in this field is P. Lambert: "Popular theatre: One road to a self-determined action", in <u>Community Development Journal</u>, 1982, No. 3.

[8] Hoxeng, op. cit.

[9] G. Huizer: <u>Preliminary guidelines for participatory monitoring and on-going evaluation of PPP</u>, draft manuscript (Rome, FAO), p. 24: FAO: <u>People's participation in rural development through the promotion of self-help organizations</u> (Rome, n.d.).

[10] Huizer, op. cit. The main duties of the agent are:

(a) to assist the agency responsible for the project in surveying the socio-economic structure of selected villages;

(b) to initiate and assist the villagers in forming small informal self-help groups;

(c) to assist the small groups in planning (determining the objectives, identifying constraints and selecting the means), income-generating activities, improvements in food production and processing and for improved social and economic infrastructure (participatory action research);

(d) to assist the small groups implement the activities they have decided to carry out;

(e) continuously to motivate the groups for self-help actions, whenever such action can lead to the solution of a problem, and stimulate self-determination;

(f) to arrange for and participate in the training of group members;

(g) to act as intermediary between the groups and the supporting agency;

(h) to assist the groups to develop into well-functioning receiving mechanism for the government extension service and enlist the support of the latter.

The ILO study refers to the SARILAKAS project in the Philippines.

[11] See, for example, Bhasin, op. cit.; F. O'Gorman: <u>Conscientization, whose initiative should it be?</u> (Rio de Janeiro, FASE, 1980); Etting, op. cit.; G.V.S. de Silva: "Bhoomi Sena: A struggle for people's power", in <u>Development dialogue</u> (1979, No. 2, pp. 3-70; B. Blair: <u>The training of development agents</u> (Reading University, unpublished dissertation, 1979).

[12] Probably the first substantial examination of the issue of the non-material objectives of rural development projects can be found in W. Haque et al.: "Towards a theory of rural development", in <u>Development dialogue</u> (1977, No. 2, pp. 113-137).

[13] Huizer, op. cit.

[14] P. Oakley: "Evaluating social development: How much of how good?" in Reading Rural Development Communications Bulletin (University of Reading), 1982, No. 14, pp. 12-18.

[15] Two of the more substantial examples of this literature are W. Haque et al.: "Towards a theory of rural development", op. cit. and B. Galjart: "Counterdevelopment: A position paper", in Community Development Journal (Oxford), 1981, No. 2.

[16] See, for example, W. Fernandes and R. Tandon (eds.): Participatory research and evaluation (New Delhi, Indian Social Institute, 1981). Also Md. A. Rahman: "The theory and practice of participatory action research" and B.L. Hall: "Participatory research popular knowledge and power" in IFDA Dossier (Nyon, International Foundation for Development Alternatives), Sep.-Oct. 1982; B. Knotts: Participatory evaluation: An educational process for social development action (Reading University, unpublished dissertion, 1979).

Chapter 5

CONCLUDING STATEMENT

The foregoing chapters have attempted to examine the ways in
which participation has been viewed and relate this examination to
a range of examples which illustrate the many dimensions which have
been labelled "participatory". As indicated in the first chapter,
with the decreased certainty attached to the direction of development, established explanations and modes of intervention no longer
appear adequate. Attempts to deal with the many intransigent
development problems have focused on such characteristics as poverty
and unemployment, but have largely failed to come to terms with the
human agents associated with the causes of such problems.

It is a two-sided struggle. On the one side it is a struggle
to secure basic needs and worth while employment for those who are
denied them and to provide value to existence and viable explanations for processes over which people feel they have little control.
On the other side it is a struggle to avoid co-option and control by
forces which imply rigidity and decreased creativity and flexibility,
because they commit people to narrower, more dogmatic and often more
oppressive forms of standardisation. There is a constant tension
between these centrifugal and centripetal tendencies, encountered
at all levels; from the "struggle" within the household between
women and men in the context of the former's attempts to emerge from
a veil of ignorance and neglect, to relationships between nations.
Such a process implies a constant questioning of the often taken-
for-granted world.

In this struggle "participation" occupies an uneasy space.[1]
As the nature of the struggle changes, so do the forms which participation takes. It is thus perhaps counterproductive to attempt
the accumulation of composite lists and guide-lines because this
merely perpetuates particular forms.[2] "Participation" therefore
must be viewed as a normative concept whose meaning changes with the
changing explanations of social processes.

A great mass of material has been produced which attempts to
formalise participation and to provide prescriptions for its
successful implementation. There seems to be general agreement
that participation is essential for development. (Some would argue
that development in fact is participation). From this assumption

arises questions about its operationalisation, on the grounds that more of it is bound to be beneficial. But can participation be perceived as if it were an ingredient to be injected into a target group? Can participation ever be institutionalised or legislated for? Obviously public commitments to its promotion and extension can be made but this does not guarantee its implementation. In the final analysis participation remains illusive. Much of what has been written is inconclusive and so general and conditional as to be unconnected with processes in the real world; either a public rhetoric which disguises an often harsh and unequal reality or so abstract as to be of little value in the search for a way forward. We cannot just proclaim participation, we must be equally concerned with its authentic implementation.

In this context a typology of levels of participation might be devised ranging from forms of intervention at the bottom which, while perhaps called "participatory", could be seen as manipulatory or as therapeutic. Mass mobilisation campaigns might be seen in this category. In the middle levels are token forms of participation associated with the extension of information, consultation and collaboration of one sort or another. At the upper levels are partnerships, delegated power and citizen control, which are regarded as "real" forms of participation.[3] Such a typology involves the investigation of obstacles to "participation" at all levels and different tools will be used at each level. This begs the question of whether these levels are mutually exclusive or not and whether people interested in pursuing the issue of participation are really thinking in terms of shared control.

We have touched in this paper upon the issue of obstacles and problems to participation but have eschewed the presentation of "lists" of such obstacles. Such lists assume that once the obstacles have been correctly identified they can be more easily removed. There is no dearth of literature which focuses on structural features of inequality as explanations for a lack of authentic participation. These are enshrined in United Nations resolutions of many sorts which call for "radical structural change". The obstacles then are located in the present structural conditions which entrench the vested interests of those already holding assets and power and who are able to operate in the name of the state or the nation. These, obviously, are likely to be the ones who are the major resisters of "radical structural change".

What if the questions that we ask and the obstacles that we thereby identify are wrong?   Competing explanations of poverty in the rural areas, on the one hand, isolate the individual and tradi- tional values as the major obstacles; while on the other hand the "system" is isolated as the major obstacle, in which individuals are subjected to unequal and oppressive forms of inter-relationships. According to which explanation one accepts will depend the nature of the policy prescription offered and the attendant programme or project elaborated.   The identification of the obstacles thus depends on the evaluative tools employed, which are inevitably con- ditioned by the perspective that the evaluation employs.   Like participation, evaluation can thus never be considered neutral.   If it is in the interests of some, it is against the interests of others.

Changing the accepted framework within which problems are perceived may do more than any other act to affect our future understanding of participation.   We reviewed in Chapter 1 the changing analysis of the causes of underdevelopment and we have suggested throughout the need to look at participation in a radi- cally different perspective.   The implication is not to abandon the existing patterns of intervention, but rather to search for more appropriate ways in which a participatory approach underlies the whole basis of the intervention.   This means a sensitisation of those involved in the organisation and administration of rural development projects and an increased flexibility in the ways in which job specifications are given and expertise is trained and recruited.   These issues we have explored as a first step in Chapter 4.

We are in fact searching for a meaningful participatory strategy and, to be successful, it must be conducted outside the confines of rigid bureaucratic structures.   It is a search which is trying to relate to the rural poor who continue marginalised from the mainstream of development.   This search implies the occupation and the expansion of a "space" in which the rural poor have an opportunity to gain something.   The search is identified with an ever-strengthening counter-debate which is examining ways in which the rural poor might achieve some effective voice.   The lead in this search is being given by agencies outside formalised government structures, such as the World Council of Churches and the major voluntary agencies.[4]   The United Nations agencies are similarly concerned with the search and, where possible, give it active support.   We have examined the conceptual basis of this search in Chapter 1, and further examined it with particular reference to participation in the other chapters.   This counter-debate suggests a more radical meaning to participation which has implications for the whole way in which rural development projects are conceived and implemented.

Whilst we would accept that some rural people have participated in the benefits of rural development projects, the overwhelming majority have not.   For them, therefore, participation is not in the first instance concerned with such benefits, but more with achieving some kind of base from which to challenge for these benefits.   We have already seen a number of different terms used to explain this preparation of a base - "empowering", "creating space", "creating assets" - and we have examined in Chapter 4 the emerging strategy which is seeking to achieve this aim.   We are left in no doubt that meaningful participation is concerned with achieving power: that is the power to influence the decisions that affect one's livelihood.

The struggle to gain increased participation is to enhance the rights of the excluded and confront the bases of established privilege.   This has as many forms as there are relationships.   In one sense it might be suggested that the forms which gain priority are those which can be pursued at the margins and/or in areas where there is no directly perceived threat to established power interests. Perhaps it is in these areas that planned intervention has been most successful.   Thus, it could be argued that successful land reform programmes are only successful when land is no longer seen as the main basis from which to derive power.   Similarly "women's programmes" are invariably judged on the basis of their ability to generate income and create additional assets; a more meaningful judgement on their effectiveness in terms of participation should be whether or not they achieve access for women to existing assets. On the other hand more hopefully these "marginal" forms do contain the seeds of change and the possibilities to nurture challenges and effective organisations which will seek participation from the existing inequitable order.

There would appear to be a widespread commitment to participation as a process of empowering, although this commitment takes a variety of forms and uses different terminologies.   We are seeking

to create countervailing power to challenge the orthodoxies of the
past and the structures which they perpetuated.   Inevitably the
process of empowering is interpreted as a challenge, and its
practice straddles the uneasy ground between legitimacy and opposition.   We cannot conceal the fact that the practice of empowering
challenges established interests and seeks to confront those forces
which oppose the rural poor's access to the means of development.
Established bureaucracies do not charitably concede participation.
This participation must result from the inexorable processes from
below.

We conclude by commenting upon the implications of the content
of our paper for the United Nations agencies.   Our brief did not
include any detailed study of the agencies and thus our comments
must be seen in that light.   It is neither our brief to tell the
agencies what they should do in terms of their support for rural
development projects.   We have examined in this paper a concept
which the agencies have done much to promote.   A substantial part
of the formal literature on participation has been sponsored by
the United Nations, and indeed the research continues.   The WCARRD
Declaration formally committed the United Nations and member Governments to a strategy for rural development based upon the active
participation of the rural population.   Our examination of some of
the practice to date inevitably highlights the relationship of the
United Nations agencies with the nature of this practice.

It would have been wrong to have written an inconclusive paper
and merely to have examined the concept of participation in an
impassive manner.   Despite the undoubted share in the benefits of
rural development projects which have accrued to the few, we cannot
agree that such sharing contributes to meaningful participation.
We conclude that the meaningful participation of the rural poor in
development is concerned with <u>direct access</u> to the resources
necessary for development and <u>some active involvement</u> and <u>influence</u>
in the decisions affecting those resources.   To participate
meaningfully implies the ability positively to influence the course
of events.   This interpretation is implicit in the strategy which
we explained in Chapter 4.   It is also a fact that the development
of this strategy is, at this moment, shared with the NGOs, and
that formalised bureaucracies if anything resist its implementation.

Where, therefore, do the United Nations agencies stand in
relation to participation as a process of empowering?   We are loathe

to answer this question from a position of ignorance on the workings of the United Nations structure. We will limit ourselves to a few brief points:

(a) although much of the United Nations literature conceputalises participation, in one way or another, in terms of <u>empowering</u> and the United Nations supports research efforts in this context, the practice is somewhat different. There is a <u>gulf</u> between the practice of meaningful participation and the United Nations' involvement in rural development;

(b) participation as empowering inevitably <u>challenges</u> existing bureaucratic structures. The United Nations agencies are obliged to work within these existing structures and "participation" is conceded on pre-established terms. These structures are in fact the basic obstacles to meaningful participation;

(c) rural development in general, and participation in particular, are <u>not</u> government prerogatives. NGOs constitute legitimate alternatives and appropriate vehicles for achieving the participation of the rural poor. But what level of support can the United Nations agencies give to the NGO activities?

We can conclude this study by suggesting two major avenues of inquiry which, in our opinion, will help us to take the next step in terms of our understanding and use of participation. We would argue that "participation" has been adequately conceptualised in the literature to provide us with sufficient working knowledge of its many dimensions. We further believe that there is a widespread enough practice of some form of participation in rural development, both within formal government structures and within the NGOs, for substantial evidence to exist upon the nature and effect of these participatory programmes and projects. We would suggest, therefore, that the next step should include two major areas of further action:

(a) a thorough and systematic documentation and description of the <u>practice</u> of participation, based on rural development projects sponsored by both government and non-government agencies. Such a systematic study would help us better to understand the <u>method</u> of participation and thus how best to promote participation in such projects;

(b) a major effort to tackle the difficult problem of the <u>monitor-</u>
     <u>ing</u> and <u>evaluation</u> of "participation". Conventional tech-
     niques of project appraisal and evaluation are inadequate for
     the qualitative process of participation, and we still lack a
     rigorous methodology for monitoring and evaluating participa-
     tion. We will be better able to promote participation if we
     can better understand its development within the context of a
     rural development project.

     To do nothing is to perpetuate a state of affairs which most
reasonable people consider to be unacceptable. But a commitment
to seek the meaningful participation of the rural poor in development will be successful only if established orthodoxies are
challenged and the paradigm well and truly shifted.

<u>Notes</u>:

     [1] The use of the term "space" in this context reflects the way
in which the term is used in the UNRISD inquiry into participation.

     [2] It could be argued that Chapter 4 in fact constitutes such
a composite list and set of guide-lines. The point we wish to
make here is that rigid adherence to such lists and guide-lines
overlooks the dynamic nature of participation, a process which
cannot be encapsulated indefinitely within prescribed boundaries.

     [3] The idea of levels of participation is derived from
S.R. Arnstein: "A ladder of citizen participation" in <u>American</u>
<u>Institute of Planners' Journal</u>, July 1969.

     [4] See, for example, Commission on the Churches Participation
in Development: <u>People's participation and people's movements</u>
(Geneva, WCC, 1981).